500

light meals

500

light meals

the only compendium of light meals you'll ever need

Deborah Gray

SELLERS
PUBLISHING

A Quintet Book

Published by Sellers Publishing, Inc.
161 John Roberts Road, South Portland, Maine 04106
Visit our Web site: www.sellerspublishing.com
E-mail: rsp@rsvp.com

ISBN: 978-1-4162-4501-8
e-ISBN: 978-1-4162-4502-5
Library of Congress Control Number: 2013941715
QTT.FLME

This book was conceived, designed, and produced by
Quintet Publishing Limited
6 Blundell Street
London N7 9BH
United Kingdom

Photographer: Ria Osborne
Food Stylist: Fern Green
Designer: Jacqui Caulton
Art Director: Michael Charles
Editor: Hazel Eriksson
Publisher: Mark Searle

10 9 8 7 6 5 4 3 2 1

Printed in China by 1010 Printing International Ltd.

contents

foreword

Some say that our health is all we have, and in many ways, it's the truth. Food is at the center of our health and can have a profound effect on us, positive or negative. Food and nutrition have been shown to affect not only our most basic health like cholesterol and lipid levels, but also our happiness and general well-being.

Cooking at home is the best way to ensure that your family eats well and you know exactly what is going in – and staying out – of your food. Meals at home also create the important custom of sitting down at the table, sharing a nourishing meal, and conversing with family and friends. Eating at the table without a tv allows you to pay closer attention to your satiety (how full you feel) and so you end up eating less overall, and much more mindfully.

Healthy cooking doesn't have to be boring or bland and labor intensive as you'll see in the next pages. *500 Light Meals* is full of satisfying, wholesome meals that don't feel like "diet food." One of the reasons fad diets don't work is that they require too much restriction or removing entire food groups all together which is simply unsustainable for the long-term. The balanced approach in this book (nothing off-limits) is the key to losing weight and keeping it off. Recipes are lightened by using less fat and sugar, low-fat dairy, and appropriate portions. One of my favorite components of this cookbook is that at the end of each section, there are variations for each recipe so you have an endless resource for healthy meals. Once you find your favorites, you can change them up according to what you have on hand or what is in season.

I know you'll enjoy these recipes as much as I do! Eat well.

Emily Dingmann, BSc
Nutritionist and blogger at www.anutritionisteats.com

introduction

500 Light Meals is a book full of delicious recipes, all of which are designed to be healthy and low in calories. It has not been written as a diet book offering a regime to follow that will end up with weight loss. Instead, *500 Light Meals* is designed to support weight maintenance and to inspire those who need to watch their food intake but do not want to count each calorie. For this reason the meals in the book are not calorie-counted. As a rough guide, however, our main courses are well under 500 calories per portion, lighter dishes are under 350, and desserts and baked goods are no more than 300 calories.

The objective behind the recipes is to provide some familiar and some new and creative meals using less fat and sugar than usual but without compromising on flavor and texture.

Healthy cooking shouldn't be onerous. The ingredients used in the book are not difficult to find. The cooking methods for the base recipes are all clearly written and the instructions simple to follow. The variations give you plenty of other options that, with a few changes to the original recipe, create a wide variety of novel low-calorie meals. These ideas are not just there to be followed, they are intended to provide a starting point for your own creativity so you can develop and extend your cooking repertoire to suit your lifestyle and your tastes.

a healthy diet

The old adage, "You are what you eat," holds true. Eating the right foods in the right quantities helps you obtain the nutrients and energy you need for a healthy life.

Two very basic guidelines have been taken into consideration for the purpose of this book: balance the number of calories consumed with the amount of energy you use, and eat a wide range of good-quality foods to ensure that you are getting all the nutrients the body requires. The first guideline requires a little self-discipline and a healthy lifestyle in which exercise plays a part. The second is solved by cooking a variety of recipes in this book each week and not snacking on bad stuff in between.

portion sizes

It is easy to cook the right foods, such as those in this book, and then to blow your good intentions by eating too much. Stick to the portion sizes recommended. If cooking for only two people, cook only half the recipe or plate up four meals and refrigerate two for the next day. That is so much better than serving at the table and finding the temptation for another helping too much to resist. If you do like to self-serve at the table, restrict this to vegetables and salad. Getting a set of slightly smaller plates is a good move too. Psychologically, eating from a full plate is more satisfying than receiving a meager-looking meal on a large plate.

use quality ingredients

The recipes in this book are made primarily with fresh ingredients, except where canned or frozen foods are used for convenience (canned tomatoes and beans, for instance).

Many recipes call for fresh (or frozen) fish, lean meat, and poultry without the skin, all of which are naturally low in calories. Always buy the best-quality fish and meat that you can afford — the better the animal husbandry, the better flavored the food. Select lean cuts of meat (unfortunately, these tend to be the more expensive cuts). Before cooking, trim all visible fat from meat and poultry and always skin poultry, as this is where a great deal of the fats and calories are to be found.

Lean meats generally perform best when cooked quickly. If they are slow-cooked, they need a tenderizing agent to be added. In this book, we use balsamic vinegar to tenderize meats, avoiding the more commonly used alcohol because it contains unnecessary calories. Many of our recipes keep the meat content relatively low — no more than 4 ounces per portion — and increase the vegetables or add beans and legumes. This method has overall health benefits, as it maintains a good protein intake while increasing the vitamin and mineral mix obtained from the vegetables. It also increases dietary fiber in the diet — a win-win solution.

The healthy eating advice is to eat at least five portions of fruit and vegetables every day. Eating a wide range of vegetables over the course of a week will help meet the body's nutrient needs. Many recipes in the book contain a mixture of protein and vegetables, and there are delicious salads and vegetable side dishes too. Buy vegetables that look really fresh and inviting whenever possible, especially if they are to be eaten raw or lightly cooked.

exploit bright flavors
Get the most flavor out of the calories you use by selecting foods with good, flavorful ingredients. For instance, most of the time Parmesan cheese has been used in this book because it has a strong, rich flavor, which means that you can use much less of it to obtain the same level of flavor as you would with considerably more of a less pungent cheese. Similarly, the bright flavors of fresh herbs earn their keep against their more reserved dried cousins. Chiles, spices, and citrus have also been used liberally to keep the recipes interesting and to compensate for losing the richer flavors found in butter and cream.

low-calorie cooking techniques

We've provided easy-to-follow cooking techniques throughout this book that will enable you to reduce calories.

reduce the fat

Most of our recipes use baking, broiling, grilling, poaching, or steaming, which use little, if any, added fat. Fats contain more calories per ounce than any other food type, so minimizing the fat is the first rule of low-calorie cooking.

One of the best ways to reduce fat in cooking is to use good-quality, heavy, non-stick pans. A good non-stick pan or skillet can almost eliminate the need for fat, so that you need no more than a touch of oil when sautéing.

Sometimes a recipe needs the flavor provided by sautéing, such as frying onions in a little oil to provide the caramel sweetness that forms the foundation of many recipes. We generally use canola oil, because it is low in saturated fats and high in the omega-3 fatty acids and other monounsaturated fats that help to promote a healthy heart. It is also almost tasteless and odorless and has a high smoke point, making it an ideal cooking oil. Olive oil has similar health benefits and contains more nutrients than canola oil; however, it has a stronger flavor and is more expensive.

Using cooking spray is another low-fat alternative. For most low-calorie sprays, each second of spray time releases about 7 calories. Compare that to 1/2 tablespoon of canola oil, which has 62 calories. If you are uncomfortable with the chemicals used in these store-bought sprays, use canola or olive oil in a mister, which will still result in a significant calorie reduction.

Finally, do not deep fry foods, ever.

full-fat and low-fat dairy products for comparison

	Amount *	Calories	Total fat (g)	Saturated fat (g)
Milk, whole	1 cup	146	7.93	4.55
Milk, 2%	1 cup	122	4.81	3.07
Milk, 1%	1 cup	102	2.37	1.54
Milk, skim	1 cup	86	0.44	0.28
Buttermilk, low-fat	1 cup	98	2.16	0.55
Sour cream	2 tbsp.	51	5	3.13
Sour cream, fat-free	2 tbsp.	18	0	0
Mozzarella cheese	1 1/2 oz.	128	9.45	5.55
Mozzarella, low-fat	1 1/2 oz.	108	6.77	4.3
Mozzarella, non-fat	1 1/2 oz.	63	0	0
Cream cheese	1 1/2 oz.	148	14.85	9.3
Cream cheese, low-fat	1 1/2 oz.	40.5	0.58	0.45
Cheddar cheese	1 1/2 oz.	171	14.09	8.96
Cheddar cheese, low-fat	1 1/2 oz.	74	2.98	1.85
Parmesan	1 tbsp.	22	1.43	0.87
Yogurt, full-fat	3 1/2 oz.	149	7.96	5.14
Yogurt, non-fat	3 1/2 oz.	137	0.44	0.28

*Based on standard serving size, USDA National Nutrient Database, Release 18

use low-fat dairy ingredients
Dairy products include milk, cream, cheese, and yogurt and are good sources of protein, calcium, vitamins, and minerals. Switching to low-fat or non-fat dairy products allows you to retain all the health benefits of these foods without consuming the saturated fats.

In most cooking, the substitution is very straightforward, except in baking. Be aware, however, that fat-reduced dairy products such as cream and sour cream are more likely to curdle during cooking than their full-fat counterparts. This can be compensated for by stirring 1 tablespoon cornstarch into each cup of cream to stabilize the mixture. Alternatively, add the cream at the very last minute and cook over a gentle heat without boiling.

Sometimes using a fat-free yogurt might leave the end result a little thin and runny. Using Greek-style fat-free yogurt is a good solution, as it is a naturally thicker product. If it is unavailable, put fat-free yogurt in a sieve lined with cheesecloth to allow some of the moisture to drain off before proceeding with the recipe.

cut down on sugar
It is possible to reduce the sugar by up to 50 percent in many classic sweet and baked recipes. Some of the sweetness will, of course, be lost, but if the recipe calls for spices, such as vanilla or cinnamon, adding a little extra can help replace the flavor.

Reducing the quantity of sugar in a recipe can leave a volume issue. In baking this can be made up by using cornstarch or non-fat milk powder, but this is very much a trial and error process; it will work better in some recipes than others.

As an alternative, there are many sugar replacements, but be cautious with them as some sugar substitutes lose their sweetness when cooked at high temperatures. Be aware, too, that they all have different levels of sweetness — some call for a like-for-like substitution, while others require you to use only half the amount of substitute as you would sugar. Some artificial sweeteners have a tangible aftertaste. Using strong flavors can mask this; one good trick is to add a teaspoon of coffee powder in a chocolate recipe or to add a little more cinnamon and nutmeg in a cookie.

There are some concerns about the safety of some sugar substitutes in the human diet, so they should be used with a little discretion. Persons suffering from diabetes should consult a medical professional regarding use of sugar and sugar substitutes in their diet.

For more information on a sugar substitute and its performance in cooking, and in baking in particular, check out the manufacturer's website. For this reason, all the recipes in the book use somewhat less sugar than in many conventional recipes but do not recommend the use of specific sugar substitutes.

Sugar-free syrups are a great way to add a little sweetness to foods without adding calories. They are not generally used in baking, but are great with fruit, in many desserts, and to add the sweetness in a sweet-and-sour main course dish.

low-calorie baking techniques
Butter is the ideal fat for baking against which other fats can be compared. Butter is not just fat; it contains water and milk solids. When using butter for a pastry crust, the water in the butter evaporates and creates tiny air pockets in the dough, which result in a crisp, flaky crust. The milk solids contain milk sugars, which brown when heating, resulting in a caramel-rich flavor and a golden color. Any pie crust made with low-fat spread or oil will

not benefit from this chemical balance; generally they contain too much water, which results in a heavier crust. There are acceptable recipes such as the one found on page 19, but they cannot mimic the butter-rich originals. Several recipes in the book use phyllo pastry, which is in itself low in fat. Traditionally phyllo is layered with butter in recipes, but by using a low-fat spray or an oil-filled mister instead, phyllo makes a deliciously crisp reduced-fat pie crust. Sadly there is really no such thing as a skinny cake — only skinny portions. The problem is that fat plays a crucial role in most baked goods and the role of fat changes depending on the baking method used. In general, its function is to optimize the aeration process necessary to produce a light texture. Reducing the fat content results in denser cakes or, worse, cakes that sink when removed from the oven. If you are substituting low-fat spreads or oil in baking recipes, the total fat content of the original recipe should not be reduced by more than 10 percent and the liquid in the recipe should be reduced to compensate for the liquid increase found in the fat.

Some baking methods get around this by using a large number of egg whites and little or no fat, resulting in a light and airy angel food cake-type confection, while the traditionally whisked sponge, used to make jelly rolls, whisks together eggs and sugar until very thick and sufficiently strong to hold the incorporated flour. Applesauce, or a prune, apricot, or peach purée, or a mashed banana may be substituted for half the fat in many cake recipes.

Eggs have had mixed press over the years, but they are a good low-calorie protein weighing in at about 85 calories per large egg. Egg yolks are relatively high in cholesterol, which has been the reason for their bad press; however the latest advice doesn't recommend limiting the number of eggs eaten if they form part of a well-balanced diet. In several of the recipes in this book, the amount of egg yolk has been reduced while the egg white numbers are retained. An egg white contains only 17 calories, no fat, and plenty of protein, so it is perfect for the calorie-conscious eater — hence the magic of soufflés and angel food cake.

basic recipes

The recipes included in this section are great additions to any home cook's repertoire. They will enable you to keep on cooking family favorites while cutting calories and fat.

low-fat cheese sauce

This is great as a basis of mac and cheese or other cheese dishes (see serving suggestions on page 18). The calories have been cut down in several ways. This method of making the white sauce base uses cornstarch as the thickening agent, cutting out the need for butter or oil. It is flavored with reduced-calorie cheddar cheese and Parmesan to get a good strong flavor from a limited amount of cheese, while the piquant taste of the mustard and celery salt make the sauce really flavorsome.

1 1/2 tbsp. cornstarch
1 tbsp. water
1 1/2 cups skim milk
1/4 cup low-fat cheddar cheese, shredded

1/4 cup Parmesan cheese, shredded
2 tsp. Dijon mustard
1/4 tsp. celery salt, or to taste
black pepper

Mix the cornstarch with a little water to make a smooth paste. In a medium saucepan, with a wooden spoon, combine the milk and the cornstarch mixture. Cook over medium heat, stirring continuously, until the sauce comes to a boil and thickens, about 3 minutes. Remove from heat, add the cheese and mustard, and continue to stir until the cheese has melted. Season to taste with the celery salt and black pepper.

Makes about 2 cups

ideas for using low-fat cheese sauce

Here are some serving suggestions for the low fat cheese sauce on page 16. These are especially good for helping kids to eat healthier.

macaroni & cheese with peas
Cook 12 ounces macaroni until just cooked. Mix with 1/2 cup cooked peas. Stir in the cheese sauce, put in a baking dish, and top with 1 sliced medium tomato. Sprinkle with 1 tablespoon Parmesan cheese and bake at 375°F for about 20 minutes until golden.

leek & ham gratin
Cut 8 medium leeks into thick slices and steam until just tender, 8–10 minutes. Put in a baking dish with 1/2 cup diced lean ham. Pour over the cheese sauce and sprinkle with paprika. Bake at 375°F for about 20 minutes until golden.

cheesy cauliflower & beans
Cut a cauliflower into flowerets and simmer until almost tender, about 8 minutes; drain and put in a baking dish with cheese sauce, 1 cup cherry tomatoes, 1 (15-ounce) can drained and rinsed pinto beans, and 2 tablespoons chopped fresh parsley. Mix together 1 tablespoon Parmesan cheese and 2 tablespoons bread crumbs, and sprinkle over the top. Bake at 375°F for about 20 minutes until golden.

cheese soufflé
Mix 1 cup cheese sauce with 2 egg yolks and 1 teaspoon paprika. Beat 4 egg whites until stiff, then carefully fold one third of the egg whites into the cheese sauce; repeat twice more. Gently transfer mixture to a greased 1 1/2-pint soufflé dish and bake at 400°F for 25–30 minutes until risen and golden brown. Serve immediately.

low-fat pastry

This method uses a little browned butter to add richness to the pastry. This pastry works well in one-crust pies. It is a little dense and high in calories to use in two-crust pies.

1 tbsp. butter
1 1/4 cups flour
1/4 tsp. salt

1/4 cup canola oil
2–3 tbsp. skim milk

Melt the butter in a very small pan (a metal measuring cup can be used) and cook for about 1 minute until it becomes a golden brown color; cool slightly.

Combine flour and salt in a bowl. Combine oil and browned butter. Add to flour mixture, then mix with a fork with just enough skim milk to form large clumps. Press into ball. Flatten to form a 5-inch circle. Roll out to a 12-inch circle between sheets of plastic wrap or parchment paper. Remove top piece of plastic wrap or paper and flip onto a greased 9-inch pie pan. Gently press in dough to fit. Remove second piece of plastic. Trim and flute by hand or with the tines of a fork.

To bake blind, line the pie crust with aluminum foil and fill with pie weights or dried beans. Bake in a 400°F oven for 12–15 minutes, remove the weights or beans, and bake for 8–10 minutes more or until the crust is lightly golden and the center is dry.

amaretto pie crust
Follow the basic recipe, but use amaretto liqueur for some or half of the milk.

Makes one 9-inch crust

low-fat mayonnaise

This cooked mayonnaise reduces the oil content dramatically, so use well-flavored olive oil.

1 tbsp. cornstarch	1/2 tsp. salt	1 egg, lightly beaten
2 tsp. dry English mustard	pinch white pepper	2 tbsp. white wine vinegar
1 tsp. sugar	3/4 cup low-fat buttermilk	1 tbsp. extra-virgin olive oil

In a small saucepan, mix together the cornstarch, mustard, sugar, salt, and white pepper. Mix to a smooth paste with a little of the buttermilk, then slowly incorporate the remaining buttermilk and the egg. Slowly bring to a simmer over low heat, stirring continuously. Once thickened, cook for another 20 seconds, then remove from the heat. Beat in the vinegar and olive oil, then put in a small bowl. Cover the surface of the mayonnaise with plastic wrap and let cool. This recipe makes about 2 cups and keeps for 3 days in the refrigerator.

curried mayonnaise
To the finished mayonnaise, add 2 teaspoons curry powder and 1 teaspoon sugar-free apricot preserves.

aïoli
Follow the basic recipe, adding 4 crushed garlic cloves and using lemon juice instead of white wine vinegar; season to taste with additional salt and black pepper.

watercress mayonnaise
Follow the basic recipe, using lemon juice instead of vinegar. Add 1 cup trimmed watercress and 1 crushed garlic clove, then purée until smooth.

chipotle mayonnaise
Follow the basic recipe, adding 1 canned, puréed chipotle chile in adobo sauce and using lime juice instead of vinegar.

breakfast

The old mantra about starting the day with a good breakfast is certainly true. This section has a few ideas on how to start your day on a healthy note without using up too many of your daily calories. Whether you have a sweet tooth in the morning, are a bacon-and-eggs sort of person, or can only face a beverage, you will find something to get you going in this section.

orange yogurt smoothie

see variations page 34

Breakfast in a glass for days when time is short! Try making this smoothie for reluctant teens who haven't got time to eat in the morning. As it uses raw eggs, it is not for the immunosuppressed or for pregnant women, but there are egg-free options in the variations. When using raw eggs, make sure they are really fresh.

1 1/4 cups non-fat or soy yogurt
2 1/2 cups good-quality orange juice,
    preferably fresh
2 fresh eggs

Put all the ingredients in a blender and process until smooth and fluffy. Alternatively, using a wire whisk, beat the eggs in a pitcher until smooth and fluffy, then beat in the yogurt, followed by the orange juice.

Pour into glasses to serve.

Makes 4 servings

oatmeal with berry compôte

see variations page 35

This is real oatmeal, not imitation, with a much better texture. It is a healthful start to the day that will keep you satisfied for hours. There are two cooking methods — one totally cooked in the morning and the other started the night before and then quickly finished in the morning.

2 cups water
2 cups 2% or 1% milk, or soy milk
1 cup steel-cut traditional oats
pinch salt

berry compôte
2 tbsp. water
2 tsp. sugar-free maple syrup
1 cup mixed frozen berries
1/2 tsp. grated lemon zest

Method one: In a medium saucepan, bring the water and milk to a boil. Stir in the oats and salt and cook, stirring, for a few minutes until thickened. Reduce the heat and simmer for 30 minutes, stirring occasionally.

Method two: Before going to bed the night before, bring the water and milk to a boil in a medium saucepan. Stir in the oats, cover, and leave in a cool place or the refrigerator overnight. In the morning, return it to a boil and simmer for 8–10 minutes, until soft and creamy.

While the oatmeal is cooking, put the water and maple syrup in a small saucepan, then add the berries and lemon zest, and cook until berries are soft. Adjust for sweetness and serve with the cooked oatmeal.

Makes 4 servings

apple & orange muffins

see variations page 36

These muffins are beautiful served warm. They are made with buttermilk, which reduces the amount of egg and (low-fat) butter used in the batter.

1 cup plus 2 tbsp. all-purpose flour
2 tsp. baking powder
1/2 tsp. salt
3/4 cup sugar or equivalent in sugar
    substitute
1 egg

1 tbsp. grated orange zest
1/2 tsp. vanilla extract
1 cup low-fat buttermilk
1/4 cup low-fat butter, melted and cooled
1 small Granny Smith apple, peeled, cored
    and finely chopped

Preheat oven to 400°F. Put 12 paper liners in a muffin pan.

Sift the flour, baking powder, and salt into a large bowl, then stir in the sugar. In a separate bowl, beat together the egg, orange zest, and vanilla until foamy. Beat in the buttermilk and the melted butter.

Make a well in the center of the dry ingredients and pour in the wet ingredients and the chopped apple. Stir just to combine. Do not overmix, as the batter should still be slightly lumpy.

Spoon the batter into the prepared muffin cups to about three quarters full. Bake for about 20 minutes until risen and golden and a toothpick inserted into the center comes out clean. Transfer the pan to a wire rack to cool for 2 minutes, then remove the muffins and serve warm.

Makes 12 muffins

ricotta & blueberry pancakes

see variations page 37

Using low-fat ingredients and whole-wheat flour, these pancakes contain fewer calories than regular pancakes. Still, go easy on the syrup.

1/2 cup all-purpose flour
1/4 cup whole-wheat pastry
    flour
1 tsp. baking powder
1/4 tsp. baking soda
pinch salt
generous pinch nutmeg

3/4 cup part-skim ricotta
    cheese
1 egg
1 egg white
3/4 cup plus 2 tbsp. low-fat
    buttermilk
1 tsp. sugar-free maple syrup

1 tsp. grated lemon zest
1/2 cup fresh or frozen (not
    thawed) blueberries
canola oil, to cook
sugar-free blueberry or maple
    syrup, to serve

Combine the flours, baking powder, baking soda, salt, and nutmeg in a bowl. In a separate bowl, whisk together the ricotta, whole egg, egg white, buttermilk, maple syrup, and lemon zest until foamy. Stir the ricotta–egg mixture into the dry ingredients until just combined. Stir in the blueberries.

Preheat a large skillet or griddle pan to high heat. Lightly grease with canola oil. Using about 3 tablespoons of batter for each pancake, pour the batter for 2 pancakes into the pan. Once the pancake bubbles and the edges begin to dry, turn the pancake over and cook the other side until golden. Set aside to keep warm. Repeat with the remaining batter. Serve with the blueberry or maple syrup.

Makes 8 pancakes

herb omelet with tomato

see variations page 38

The classic French omelet *fines herbes* couldn't be simpler or have brighter flavors. Don't be tempted to substitute dried herbs in this recipe, and do use your favorite fresh ones.

2 eggs
1 egg white
2 tbsp. water
1 tbsp. fresh chives, thinly sliced
1/2 tbsp. fresh parsley, chopped

1/2 tbsp. fresh chervil, chopped
1 tsp. fresh tarragon, chopped
salt and black pepper
1 tsp. low-fat butter, to cook
1 large tomato, skinned, seeded, and chopped

Preheat broiler.

Break the eggs into a small bowl, add the egg white, and beat with a fork until smooth. Stir in the water and herbs, and season generously with salt and pepper.

Melt the butter in a medium ovenproof skillet, tilting to coat the bottom of the pan with melted butter. Pour in the beaten eggs and stir gently at the edge of the pan, drawing the mixture from the sides to the center. When the egg has almost set on the top, remove from the heat. Put the chopped tomato along the center, then put pan under a hot broiler for about 3 minutes to just set. Fold a third of the omelet into the center, followed by the opposite side. Cut in half and slide onto warmed plates.

Makes 2 servings

spicy ham & egg cups

see variations page 39

Here's a great way to have a full bacon and egg breakfast while keeping an eye on the calories. Not only does prosciutto have under 20 calories per thin slice, the baking process adds very little by way of extra calories. Make this for guests and impress!

6 small thin slices prosciutto or other
   air-dried ham
1/2 ball (4 oz.) low-fat mozzarella, torn
3 tbsp. spicy salsa

1 1/2 tbsp. chopped fresh cilantro
6 eggs
salt and black pepper
fresh chile slices, to garnish (optional)

Preheat oven to 375°F. Spray a 6-cup muffin pan with low-fat cooking spray.

Line each muffin cup with a slice of prosciutto or ham. It doesn't matter if it tears, but ensure that the whole cup is covered. Sprinkle with the torn mozzarella. Top each cup with 1/2 tablespoon salsa, and sprinkle with a little cilantro.

Carefully break an egg into each cup and season with salt and pepper. Bake for 12 minutes for a lightly cooked egg and up to 17 minutes for a well-set egg. Sprinkle chopped chile slices, if using, and a little more cilantro over the eggs to serve.

Makes 6 servings

variations

orange yogurt smoothie

see base recipe page 23

banana yogurt drink
Follow the basic recipe, using 1 ripe banana instead of the eggs. For
added protein, add 1–2 scoops protein powder, according to the
manufacturer's directions.

pineapple yogurt smoothie
Follow the basic recipe, using pineapple juice instead of orange juice.

fresh fruit smoothie
Follow the basic recipe, using just 1 egg. Add to the blender 1 cup fresh fruit
such as peaches, mango, or strawberries, and 1/2 cup skim milk. Sweeten as
necessary with honey or sugar-free maple syrup.

orange yogurt smoothie with wheat germ
Follow the basic recipe, adding 1 tablespoon wheat germ to the blender
when making the smoothie.

variations

oatmeal with berry compôte

see base recipe page 25

cinnamon–raisin oatmeal
Follow the basic recipe, adding 1 teaspoon cinnamon with the oats.
Five minutes before the end of cooking, add 1/2 cup raisins. Instead of
the compôte, serve with a little sugar-free maple syrup.

oatmeal with peach compôte
Make the oatmeal as directed. For the compôte, heat 1 large sliced peach in
a saucepan with 1/4 cup peach and orange nectar, 1/2 teaspoon ground
cinnamon, and a grating of nutmeg. Sweeten with sugar-free maple syrup.

oatmeal with apple compôte
Make the oatmeal as directed. For the compôte, melt 1 teaspoon low-fat
butter in a skillet, and add 2 peeled, cored, and chopped medium Granny
Smith apples. Add 1/2 cup apple juice, 1/2 teaspoon apple pie spice, and
1 tablespoon sugar-free maple syrup, or to taste. Bring to a boil, simmer,
and cook for 5 minutes or until the apples are tender.

cranberry–orange oatmeal
Follow the basic recipe, adding 1/2 teaspoon cinnamon with the oats.
Five minutes before the end of cooking, add 1/2 cup dried cranberries and
1 teaspoon grated orange zest.

variations

apple & orange muffins

see base recipe page 26

orange & cranberry muffins
Follow the basic recipe, using 1/2 cup dried cranberries instead of the apple.

orange & chocolate chip muffins
Follow the basic recipe, using 1/2 cup semisweet chocolate chips instead of
the apple.

orange poppy seed muffins
Follow the basic recipe, using 2 tablespoons poppy seeds instead of
the apple. Sprinkle 1 teaspoon poppy seeds over the tops of the muffins
before baking.

orange & grape nut muffins
Follow the basic recipe, using 1/3 cup Grape Nuts cereal instead of the apple
and adding 2 tablespoons chopped crystallized orange peel.

variations

ricotta & blueberry pancakes

see base recipe page 29

ricotta & pear cinnamon pancakes
Follow the basic recipe, using 1/2 teaspoon cinnamon instead of the
nutmeg, and 1/2 cup finely chopped pear, either fresh or canned, instead
of the blueberries.

ricotta & orange raisin pancakes
Follow the basic recipe, using 2 teaspoons orange zest instead of the lemon
zest, and 1/2 cup raisins instead of the blueberries.

ricotta pancakes
Follow the basic recipe, using all-purpose flour instead of the whole wheat
flour and omitting the blueberries.

ricotta & blueberry pancakes with blueberry-lemon compôte
Follow the basic recipe. Make a compôte by putting 2 tablespoons water
and 1 tablespoon sugar-free maple syrup in a small saucepan, then adding
1 cup frozen blueberries and 1 teaspoon grated lemon zest and cooking
until the berries are soft and bursting. Adjust for sweetness and serve with
the pancakes.

variations

herb omelet with tomato

see base recipe page 30

herb omelet with goat cheese
Follow the basic recipe, adding 2 ounces goat cheese with the tomato.

mexican omelet
Follow the basic recipe, using 1 tablespoon chopped fresh cilantro instead
of the chervil and tarragon, and adding 1 chopped jalapeño chile. With the
tomato, add 2 tablespoons each chopped red bell pepper and red onion and
1 tablespoon chopped cilantro and paprika or cayenne to taste. Top the
folded omelet with 2 tablespoons non-fat sour cream.

herb omelet with turkey ham
Follow the basic recipe, adding 4 slices thin-cut turkey ham, cut into strips,
before adding the tomato.

herb omelet with mushrooms
Heat 1 teaspoon canola oil in the skillet and cook 1/2 cup sliced cremini
mushrooms for about 2 minutes, until soft. Remove the mushrooms and
keep warm. Cook omelet as directed, topping it with the mushrooms instead
of the tomato.

spicy ham & egg cups

see base recipe page 33

ham, egg & mushroom cups
Prepare the cups as directed, omitting the salsa. Heat a skillet, spray it with low-fat cooking spray, and cook 1 chopped small red onion for 3 minutes, then add 1/2 cup chopped mushrooms and cook until just soft. Divide this mixture between the cups and bake as directed.

ham, egg & tomato cups
Prepare the cups as directed, using 6 thick plum tomato slices instead of the salsa. Basil may be used instead of cilantro. Garnish with chopped, rehydrated sun-dried tomato.

lower calorie scrambled egg & ham cups
Beat together 3 eggs and 3 egg whites, 1 1/2 tablespoons skim milk, and salt and pepper to taste. Stir in 1 chopped green onion and the salsa. Pour this mixture into the ham-lined cups and bake until set, 15 to 20 minutes.

ham, scrambled egg & spinach cups
Prepare the scrambled egg variation above, adding 1/4 cup defrosted and drained chopped frozen spinach to the egg mixture before cooking. Bake until set, 15 to 20 minutes.

appetizers

What you want at the beginning of a meal is a
taste teaser, something to whet the appetite and
get the meal going with a sensation. We know that
you will enjoy these recipes so much that you won't
just eat them as appetizers. Several make excellent
light lunches or snacks for a cocktail party too.

eggplant dip

see variations page 53

Known as "baba ghanoush" in the Middle East, this is one of the mainstays of the mezze platter along with a mix of other spicy and bean-based salads. Whether or not it is made with tahini paste is debated across the region and from family to family. If you love the taste of tahini, check out the variations.

2 medium eggplants
2 garlic cloves, minced
1 tsp. grated lemon zest
2 tbsp. lemon juice
2 tbsp. olive oil

2 tbsp. fresh parsley, chopped
2 tbsp. fresh mint, chopped
salt and black pepper
lemon zest strips, to garnish

pomegranate seeds or
    ground sumac, to garnish
4 pita breads, warmed and cut
    into strips, to serve

Preheat oven to 400°F. Line a roasting pan with aluminum foil.

Wash and dry the eggplants, prick all over with a fork, put in the pan, and cook in oven for 25–40 minutes, depending on size. The idea is to completely blacken the skin of the eggplant; it doesn't matter if it splits during the process.

Strip the skin off the eggplant, retaining any flesh stuck to it, and discard. Cut the eggplant in half and, with your fingers, divide into long strips. Drain the flesh in a colander for 1 hour and discard the resulting excess liquid. Roughly chop the eggplant flesh and place in a bowl with the garlic, lemon zest, and juice, oil, parsley, mint, and salt and pepper. Stir well, then let sit for at least 1 hour. Serve at room temperature garnished with fine strips of lemon zest and pomegranate seeds or ground sumac. Serve with warmed pita strips.

Makes 4 servings

salmon wraps with cheesy shrimp filling

see variations page 54

These are pretty as a picture. Salmon is full of omega-3 fatty acids, the "healthy" fats that carry a host of beneficial properties. With 99 calories in a three-ounce serving, smoked salmon earns its keep in anyone's books.

filling
4 large cooked shrimp, deveined and
    finely chopped
3/4 cup low-fat cream cheese
1/4 cup celery, finely chopped
3 tbsp. cucumber, finely chopped
1 green onion, finely chopped

1 tsp. lemon juice
1 tbsp. fresh dill, chopped
salt and black pepper

4 slices smoked salmon
watercress, to serve
fresh dill fronds and lemon wedges, to garnish

Combine all the ingredients for the filling in a small bowl, and season to taste.

Lay the slices of smoked salmon flat on a board. Put one quarter of the filling in the center of each slice. Wrap the salmon over the filling, like wrapping a present. Sprinkle a little watercress on each serving plate, top with the salmon parcel, folded-side down, then garnish with dill fronds and lemon wedges.

Makes 4 servings

moules marinière

see variations page 55

This classic French dish is often made with wine or hard apple cider. This recipe reduces the quantities used, thereby losing calories without compromising on taste. It looks impressive, but it is so simple to put together.

2 1/4 lbs. fresh mussels in the shell (or frozen
    cooked mussels in the shell, defrosted)
1 onion, sliced
1 garlic clove, minced
1/2 cup dry white wine

3/4 cup fish broth
1/2 teaspoon peppercorns
1 bay leaf
2 tbsp. fresh parsley, chopped
1 lemon, halved

Wash or scrub the mussels and discard any that have broken shells. Tap any open mussels; if they don't close, discard. Pull away and discard the "beard" on the shell.

Put the mussels, onion, garlic, wine, broth, peppercorns, bay leaf, and half the parsley in a saucepan. Cut the lemon in half, squeeze the juice into the pan, and then add the lemon halves. Bring to a boil. Cover with a tightly fitting lid and cook over high heat until the mussels are open — about 3 minutes. Frozen mussels should open the same as fresh ones.

Divide the mussels between warmed serving bowls, discarding any that haven't opened. Discard the bay leaf and lemon halves. Strain the hot cooking liquor over the mussels and serve immediately, garnished with remaining parsley.

Makes 4 servings

salt & black pepper potato chips with tomato salsa

see variations page 56

An ingenious way to make chips in the microwave. A serving of these chips will be around 130 calories. Timings vary according to microwave power and thickness of slices.

tomato salsa
1 lb. ripe tomatoes, finely chopped
1/2 red bell pepper, finely chopped
1/2 red onion, finely chopped
2 green onions, finely sliced

1 small jalapeño chile, seeded and chopped
2 tbsp. lime juice
1/4 tsp. sugar
1/4 cup fresh cilantro, chopped
salt and black pepper

chips
1 lb. small red potatoes, washed
1 1/2 tsp. canola oil
1/2 tsp. sea salt
black pepper

Combine all the ingredients for the salsa in a bowl and let sit at room temperature. Slice the potatoes to no more than 1/8-inch thick, using either a sharp knife or a mandoline. Put slices in a bowl of cold water and let sit for 30 minutes. Do not omit this step. Drain the potatoes and dry on a paper towel. Put the oil, salt, and several grindings of black pepper in a bowl; toss in the potatoes; and turn to coat evenly. Line the microwave plate with baking parchment and spray with low-fat cooking spray. Arrange about half of the potatoes in a single layer on the parchment and microwave on high for 2–3 minutes. Turn and cook for another 2–3 minutes. You will need to check the chips regularly during the second phase, moving them around to prevent scorching. Transfer to a plate lined with paper towels and let cool. The chips will crisp up further as they cool. Repeat with the remaining potatoes.

Makes 4 servings

southern crab cakes with pineapple watercress salsa

see variations page 57

A great summertime favorite, these crab cakes freeze well before cooking, so double the recipe and freeze some for another day.

crab cakes
8 oz. crabmeat, fresh or frozen
    and thawed
1 egg white
1 garlic clove, minced
3 tbsp. red bell pepper,
    finely chopped
1 green onion, finely sliced
1 tbsp. low-fat mayonnaise
1/2 tbsp. Dijon mustard

zest of 1/2 lemon
1 tbsp. fresh parsley, chopped
    or 1 tsp. dried
1 tsp. paprika or seafood
    seasoning
salt and black pepper
1/4 cup bread crumbs

1 tbsp. canola oil or low-fat
    vegetable spray, to cook

salsa
1 1/2 cups fresh or canned
    pineapple, chopped
1/2 bunch watercress,
    chopped
1/2 small red onion, chopped
1/2–1 jalapeño chile, seeded
    and chopped
1 tbsp. lime juice
salt and black pepper

In a bowl, combine all the ingredients for the crab cakes, using clean hands or a wooden spoon. Form into 8 small crab cakes. Heat half the oil or low-fat spray in a skillet and cook half of the crab cakes over medium heat for 3–4 minutes each side, or until golden brown. Remove from pan, drain on paper towels, and keep warm. Repeat with the remaining crab cakes, adding more oil or spray to the skillet, as required.

While the crab cakes are cooking, combine all the ingredients for the salsa. Serve with the crab cakes.

Makes 8 crab cakes

asparagus summer rolls with hoisin chili dipping sauce

see variations page 58

Using spring roll wrappers makes this Vietnamese specialty a beautiful and unusual appetizer.

hoisin chili dipping sauce
1/4 cup hoisin sauce
1/4 cup water
3 tbsp. chili garlic sauce
1 tbsp. soy sauce
2 tsp. cider vinegar
1 tsp. honey

1 tsp. shredded fresh
   ginger

summer rolls
24 thin asparagus spears
8 (8-inch) spring roll
   wrappers

4 red lettuce leaves, shredded
1 cup bean sprouts
1 medium carrot, julienned
6 radishes, sliced
1 red chile, seeded and sliced
   (optional)
1/4 cup chopped fresh mint

Combine all the ingredients for the dipping sauce and let sit at room temperature. Taste and adjust for sweetness. Let stand while preparing the rolls.

Steam the asparagus until tender-crisp; cool. Submerge the spring roll wrappers in warm water for about 30 seconds until flexible, then lay out on a board. Prepare the rest of the filling ingredients.

Put one quarter of the filling ingredients in the center of each wrapper roll, placing the asparagus first to ensure that it is on the top of the roll. Fold over the ends, then firmly roll up to seal in the contents. Cut in half and serve with the dipping sauce.

Makes 4 servings

polenta canapés with antipasto

see variations page 59

These are deceptively easy to conjure up and they are absolutely delicious. There are lots of different types of antipasto in gourmet food shops; this is a great way to serve them.

1/2 (24-oz.) package prepared polenta
4 tsp. sun-dried tomato paste
16 fresh basil leaves

1 cup mixed antipasto in brine,
    from a jar
2 tbsp. Parmesan shavings

Preheat broiler to high.

Cut the polenta into 1/3-inch slices. Put on a broiler pan and spray once with low-fat olive oil-flavored cooking spray. Broil for 2–3 minutes to crisp; turn, spray, and cook for another 2 minutes on the second side. If liked, score the top side of the polenta with a heated skewer for decoration.

Put the antipasto in a food processor and pulse a few times to roughly chop into corn kernel-sized pieces. Spread the polenta with sun-dried tomato paste, leaving a small margin around the edges. Top each one with 2 basil leaves, and then add the chopped antipasto.

Sprinkle with a few Parmesan shavings.

Makes 8 canapés

stuffed mushrooms

see variations page 60

These crunchy stuffed mushrooms are guaranteed to please everyone. Be sure not to overcook them — biting into a moist mushroom is part of their charm.

8 oz. baby spinach
12 large cremini mushrooms,
   stalks removed
6 slices prosciutto, or other air-dried ham,
   visible fat removed, chopped
1/4 cup fresh bread crumbs
1 tsp. olive oil

1 tsp. dried Italian herbs
1 tsp. sweet paprika
1 tsp. lemon zest
3 tbsp. Parmesan cheese or
   reduced-fat cheddar cheese, shredded
olive oil–flavored low-fat cooking spray

Preheat oven to 400°F. Spray a cookie sheet with olive oil-flavored low-fat cooking spray. Put the spinach in a colander and pour a kettle of boiling water over it to wilt. Drain, let cool, squeeze out excess liquid, and chop.

Wipe the mushroom caps and stems with damp paper towels. Set the caps aside. Roughly chop the stems. Put chopped mushrooms in a bowl and add the spinach, ham, bread crumbs, olive oil, herbs, paprika, lemon zest, and half of the cheese. Use the filling to stuff the mushroom caps.

Put stuffed caps on the prepared cookie sheet and sprinkle with the remaining cheese. Spray with olive oil-flavored low-fat cooking spray. Bake for 15–20 minutes and serve while hot.

Makes 12 stuffed mushrooms

chicken pâté with capers & green peppercorns

see variations page 61

This is a deliciously rich pâté that freezes well, so make double the quantity to have as a standby. It is delicious served with fig or pear slices.

3 strips bacon
8 oz. chicken livers
2/3 cup chicken broth
1 garlic clove
1 small onion, chopped

1 bay leaf
1/2 tsp. dried thyme
1/4 tsp. dry mustard
1 tbsp. reduced-fat
   butter

1 tbsp. green peppercorns
1 tsp. capers, chopped
crackers or melba toast,
   to serve

Dry-fry the bacon in a small skillet until crisp. Drain on paper towels.

Meanwhile, put the chicken livers, broth, garlic, onion, bay leaf, and thyme in a pan. Bring to a boil, then simmer for 10–15 minutes until the chicken livers are cooked through. Drain, reserving the liquor. Remove and discard the garlic clove and bay leaf; cool slightly.

Put the chicken liver mixture, bacon, mustard, butter, and 3 tablespoons of the reserved cooking liquor in a food processor. Blend until smooth and creamy, adding more liquid as necessary to achieve a thick consistency. Stir in the capers and peppercorns. Season to taste with salt and pepper. Put in a serving bowl and serve with crackers or melba toast.

Makes 8 servings

variations

eggplant dip

see base recipe page 41

eggplant & tahini dip
Follow the basic recipe. Beat 1/4 cup tahini with the lemon juice and oil, adding 1 tablespoon water to make a smooth paste. Add to the eggplant with the remaining ingredients.

creamy eggplant dip
Follow the basic recipe, using only 1 tablespoon olive oil. Stir 1/4 cup non-fat Greek yogurt into the dip.

smooth & silky eggplant dip
Follow the basic recipe, but after the eggplant flesh has been drained, process until smooth in a food processor before combining with remaining ingredients.

spicy eggplant & roasted tomato dip
Follow the basic instructions, roasting 1 cup cherry tomatoes at the same time as the eggplant. When cool enough to handle, slip out of their skins and roughly chop. Add to the dip with 2–4 teaspoons harissa paste.

variations

salmon wraps with cheesy shrimp filling

see base recipe page 42

salmon wraps with tzatziki
Follow the basic recipe, using a tzatziki filling. Combine 1 cup non-fat Greek yogurt; 1 mini cucumber, peeled and finely diced; 1 small garlic clove, minced; 1 tablespoon lemon juice; 1 tablespoon fresh mint; and salt and black pepper to taste. Let sit for 30 minutes before using.

salmon pinwheels
Follow the basic recipe, laying the smoked salmon strips on the work surface. Spread with the filling, leaving 1 inch at one short end. Roll up tightly, slice and arrange the rolls on a serving platter.

salmon wraps with olives & capers
Follow the basic recipe, using an olive–caper filling. Combine 1 cup low-fat ricotta cheese, 2/3 cup sliced pimento-stuffed olives, 2 tablespoons capers, and 1 tablespoon chopped chives.

prosciutto wraps with cheesy shrimp filling
Follow the basic recipe, replacing the salmon with 12 small, thin slices prosciutto or other air-dried ham. Overlap 3 slices on a board and wrap as with the salmon parcels.

variations

moules marinière

see base recipe page 45

creamy moules with tarragon
Follow the basic recipe, replacing the parsley with fresh tarragon. Add
1/2 cup low-fat cream substitute to the cooking liquid once the mussels
are cooked, and heat through.

moules with cider
Follow the basic recipe, using hard cider instead of white wine. Add 1 slice
smoked ham, stripped of all visible fat and chopped into small pieces. Also
add 2 tablespoons low-fat cream substitute just before serving, if liked.

chili moules
Follow the basic recipe, adding 1 fresh whole red chile, 1 teaspoon
Worcestershire sauce, a few drops Tabasco sauce, and 1 sprig fresh thyme to
the saucepan with the onions.

moules frites
Prepare a portion of baked fries (page 156). Have the mussels prepared and
in the pan with the other ingredients. Five minutes before the fries are
finished, begin to cook the mussels. Serve with a communal bowl of fries.

variations

salt & black pepper potato chips with tomato salsa

see base recipe page 46

low-fat sweet potato chips

Follow the basic recipe, using sweet potatoes instead of red potatoes.
Sprinkle 1/2 teaspoon brown sugar over each batch before cooking and add
a light dusting of cinnamon halfway through the cooking time. Serve with
non-fat sour cream instead of salsa.

low-fat chips with lemon coriander salt & tomato salsa

Follow the basic recipe, replacing sea salt with lemon coriander salt. Put
2 tablespoons sea salt flakes in a small non-stick skillet over high heat and
cook until they begin to change color, about 4 minutes. Add 1/2 tablespoon
coriander seeds and 1/4 teaspoon lemon zest and cook for a further minute.
Grind with a pestle and mortar; cool. This recipe works with other spices
such as fennel or cumin seeds.

low-fat beet & parsnip chips with tomato salsa

Follow the basic recipe, replacing the potatoes with 8 ounces each of peeled,
sliced beet and parsnip. Cook the beet in one batch and the parsnip in another.

low-fat salt & black pepper potato chips with italian salsa

Follow the basic recipe for the salsa, but use lemon juice instead of lime
juice and basil instead of cilantro. Add 1/4 cup quartered olives.

southern crab cakes with pineapple watercress salsa

see base recipe page 47

ginger crab cakes with pineapple watercress salsa

Follow the basic recipe, adding 1 tablespoon shredded fresh ginger and a few drops Tabasco sauce to the crabmeat.

crab & shrimp cakes with pineapple watercress salsa

Follow the basic recipe, using 4 ounces crabmeat and 4 ounces raw, peeled, and deveined shrimp, chopped into small pieces.

smoked salmon cakes with pineapple watercress salsa

Follow the basic recipe, using 6 ounces flaked cooked salmon and 2 ounces chopped smoked salmon instead of crabmeat.

supper-sized crab cake with pineapple watercress salsa

Double the basic recipe and use a 1/4-cup measure to form the mixture into 4 crab cakes. Cook for 3–5 minutes on each side.

variations

asparagus summer rolls with hoisin chili dipping sauce

see base recipe page 48

salmon asparagus summer rolls with hoisin chili dipping sauce
Follow the basic recipe, adding 2 small cooked and flaked salmon fillets to the summer roll. Omit the radish and use 1/2 cup peeled and julienned cucumber.

asparagus summer rolls with nuoc cham dipping sauce
Prepare the summer rolls. For the dipping sauce, combine juice of 1 lemon and 1 lime, 1/4 cup water, 3 tablespoons fish sauce, 2 tablespoons sugar or sugar substitute, 3 minced garlic cloves, and 1 thinly sliced bird's eye chile.

jumbo shrimp summer rolls with peanut dipping sauce
Follow the basic recipe, omitting the asparagus and using 24 cooked, peeled, and deveined jumbo shrimp, sliced in half horizontally. Arrange them so they are on top of the finished roll. For a nutty dressing, add up to 3 tablespoons reduced-fat crunchy peanut butter to the dipping sauce.

asparagus summer rolls with bean thread noodles & hoisin chili dipping sauce
Follow the basic recipe, adding to the filling 2 ounces bean thread noodles cooked in boiling water or as directed on the package, then cooled. These can be added to any of the variations.

polenta canapés with antipasto

see base recipe page 50

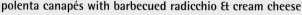

polenta canapés with barbecued radicchio & cream cheese

Cut 1/2 head radicchio in half, remove core. Put under the broiler, spray
once with cooking spray, and season with salt and pepper. Broil for about
3 minutes until just beginning to brown. Chop into bite-size pieces.
Prepare the polenta cakes as directed and spread with tomato paste. Top
with radicchio and 1 teaspoon low-fat cream cheese per canapé. Put back
under broiler for 1 minute, or serve at room temperature.

polenta cakes with tapenade

Follow the basic recipe, using 1 1/2 teaspoons tapenade per canapé instead
of antipasto. Garnish each canapé with a slice of hard-boiled egg.

polenta cakes margherita

Follow the basic recipe, omitting antipasto. Top instead with 1 slice ripe
tomato and half of a mini mozzarella ball. Put under the broiler for 1–2
minutes to heat through if serving hot, or serve at room temperature.

polenta cakes with cream cheese & salmon

Prepare the basic polenta cakes, omitting topping ingredients. Top with
1/4 cup fat-free cream cheese and 1/4 cup smoked salmon pieces. Top each
canapé with a few drops lemon juice and a grinding of black pepper. Garnish
with chopped fresh dill.

variations

stuffed mushrooms

see base recipe page 51

crab-stuffed mushrooms

Follow the basic recipe, using a crabmeat filling. Combine 1/2 cup fat-free cream cheese, 3 ounces crabmeat, 1 minced garlic clove, 1 sliced green onion, and salt and pepper to taste.

vegetarian-stuffed mushrooms

Follow the basic recipe, omitting the ham. Use instead 2 tablespoons each of finely chopped sun-dried tomatoes and black olives.

tex-mex stuffed mushrooms

Follow the basic recipe, using a Tex-Mex stuffing. Dry-fry 4 ounces lean ground beef in a skillet. Add 1/4 cup salsa verde (from a jar) and 1/4 cup fat-free sour cream. Fill caps, then top with 2 tablespoons shredded low-fat cheddar cheese.

spiced turkey-stuffed mushrooms

Follow the basic recipe, replacing the stuffing with 1 cup of mixture for Persian spiced turkey loaf (page 193).

variations

chicken pâté with capers & peppercorns

see base recipe page 52

chicken pâté with cranberries
Follow the basic recipe, omitting capers and peppercorns. Rehydrate
2 tablespoons dried cranberries in 1/4 cup boiling water, drain, and cool.
Chop and add to the pâté. Lay a line of dried cranberries decoratively on the
top of the pâté.

duck & orange pâté
Follow the basic recipe, using 8 ounces duck liver instead of chicken livers
and omit capers and peppercorns. When puréeing, add only 2 tablespoons
of the reserved liquor and add 1 tablespoon orange juice and 1 teaspoon
orange zest.

creamy chicken & sage pâté
Follow the basic recipe, omitting capers, peppercorns, and thyme. Instead
use 1 tablespoon chopped fresh sage or 1 teaspoon dried sage. Replace the
butter with 1/2 cup low-fat cream cheese. Garnish the finished pâté by
pressing whole sage leaves into the top.

veal & cranberry pâté
Follow the basic recipe, replacing the chicken livers with 8 ounces trimmed
calves' liver cut into 1/2-inch-thick slices. Rehydrate 1/4 cup dried
cranberries in boiling water for 5 minutes, drain, and add to the pâté instead
of capers and peppercorns.

little meals

There are times when a small meal is all that's
required, whether it's lunchtime or a Sunday
evening after a late brunch. The following recipes
provide a mouthwatering selection for eating in or
taking out. What's true for all of them is that they
are packed full of flavor, not calories!

crustless quiche

see variations page 80

Avoid unwanted calories with this skinny quiche that uses sliced zucchini instead of pastry. Serve straight from the plate, hot or cold, as the zucchini crust doesn't hold together as solidly as a regular crust.

2 large zucchini, thinly sliced
6 oz. mushrooms, very finely chopped
4 green onions, finely sliced
1 tsp. dried thyme
2 eggs

1 egg white
2/3 cup 1% milk or soy milk
1 tsp. Worcestershire sauce
salt and black pepper
1 tomato, sliced

Preheat oven to 350°F.

Spray a 6-inch pie plate with low-fat spray. Line the base and sides of the pan with the zucchini slices, overlapping them slightly. Sprinkle the mushrooms, green onions, and parsley over the zucchini.

Lightly beat together the eggs, egg white, and milk, then stir in the thyme, Worcestershire sauce, and salt and pepper to taste. Pour over the mushrooms and onions. Decorate with the sliced tomato.

Bake for 35–40 minutes, or until the filling is firm to touch. Serve hot or cold.

Makes 4–6 servings

asparagus with poached egg

see variations page 81

Take advantage of asparagus in season to make this classic dish. It's a perfect choice for brunch or light lunch.

1 bunch asparagus, ends trimmed
2 tsp. vinegar
2 fresh eggs

3 tbsp. Parmesan shavings
salt and black pepper

Bring lightly salted water in a large deep skillet to a boil. Add the asparagus and cook for about 5 minutes until just tender. Drain and keep warm.

At the same time, bring a saucepan of water to a boil, add the vinegar, and reduce the heat to medium-low to keep the water barely simmering. Crack an egg into a cup. Stir the water with a spoon to create a whirlpool. Carefully slip the egg into the center of the whirlpool and cook for 4 minutes or until done to your liking. Use a slotted spoon to transfer to a warm plate, cover, and keep warm. Repeat with the remaining egg.

Divide the asparagus between 2 serving plates, top with an egg, season with salt and pepper, then sprinkle with Parmesan. Serve immediately.

Makes 2 servings

turkey & water chestnut lettuce wraps

see variations page 82

As the they are constructed at the table, these deliciously healthy wraps make a fun lunch.

1 tsp. canola oil or low-fat cooking spray
8 oz. ground turkey
1/2 tsp. fresh ginger, minced
1/2 tsp. garlic, minced
1 small carrot, thickly shredded
2 green onions, sliced

1/2 (8-oz.) can water chestnuts, chopped
3 tbsp. teriyaki sauce
iceberg lettuce leaves
1/2 red bell pepper, thinly sliced
2 tbsp. fresh cilantro, chopped
hoisin sauce, for dipping

Heat the oil or spray in a wok or large skillet and stir-fry the ground turkey, garlic, and ginger until the turkey is cooked through, about 5 minutes. Add the carrots and stir-fry for about 1 minute, then add the green onions and water chestnuts and stir-fry for another minute. Add the teriyaki sauce and cook for 2 minutes.

Transfer the stir-fry to a large platter and serve alongside the lettuce, bell peppers, and cilantro. Allow everyone to construct their own wrap with hoisin sauce on the side for dipping.

Makes 2 servings

minted feta parcels

see variations page 83

These little triangles are delicious served with a tomato and onion salad. The first
triangle may seem a little difficult to construct, but after that, the rest are really simple.

12 oz. fresh spinach or 4 oz. frozen leaf spinach
2 tsp. canola oil or low-fat cooking spray
1 small onion, sliced
4 oz. feta cheese, crumbled
1 tsp. dried mint

salt and black pepper
6 (9x14-in.) sheets phyllo pastry
low-fat cooking spray for layering
1 tbsp. sesame seeds

Preheat oven to 375°F. Line a cookie sheet with baking parchment.

For fresh spinach, wilt it in boiling water for a couple of minutes, then drain. If frozen,
defrost gently, then drain. Press out excess liquid, then roughly chop. Heat the oil or spray in
a skillet, add the onion, and cook gently for about 5 minutes until softened, stirring
occasionally. Stir into the spinach with the feta and mint.

Lightly spray a phyllo sheet with oil. Top with a second sheet, spray with oil, then add third
sheet and spray. Cut pastry stack in half lengthwise. Spoon a quarter of the spinach mixture
onto the short end of a pastry strip. Fold pastry over to form a triangle. Continue to fold
until filling is enclosed. Place on prepared cookie sheet. Repeat with remaining pastry and
spinach mixture. Spray the tops of the pastries and sprinkle with sesame seeds. Bake for
15–20 minutes or until pastry is golden.

Makes 2 large or 4 small servings

garbanzo burgers with lemon tahini dressing

see variations page 84

These burgers are based on a traditional falafel mixture, shaped into a burger. You can serve them with a mixed salad or stuffed in a pita bread.

1 small carrot
3/4 cup garbanzo beans
1 tbsp. garbanzo flour or
   whole wheat flour
1/2 red bell pepper
1 green onion, trimmed
1/2 tsp. dried chili flakes
1 1/2 tbsp. tahini
2 tsp. lemon juice

1/4 tsp. ground cumin
pinch cayenne pepper
1 tbsp. fresh cilantro, chopped
salt and black pepper
2 tsp. toasted sesame seeds
egg white, lightly beaten, or 1
   1/2 tbsp. ground flaxseeds
canola oil or low-fat cooking
   spray

dressing
2 tbsp. tahini
1/4 tsp. garlic paste
2 tbsp. lemon juice
2 tbsp. water
1/8 tsp. salt
pinch cayenne pepper
1 tbsp. fresh parsley, chopped

Put the carrot in a food processor and process until finely chopped. Add the next 10 ingredients and pulse to combine. Season with salt and pepper. Stir in the sesame seeds and sufficient egg white or flaxseeds to bind. Form the mixture in your hands into 4 small or 2 large patties. Heat the oil or spray in a heavy skillet over medium heat, add patties, cover, and cook over low-moderate heat for about 10 minutes, until the bottoms begin to brown. Flip patties and cook the second side for 8 minutes, or until golden.

Meanwhile, combine dressing ingredients in a small bowl and whisk with a fork.

Makes 2 large or 4 small servings

zucchini & ricotta fritters

see variations page 85

These fritters are delicious with a green salad or, on cooler days, with broiled tomatoes. Add a slice of lean ham or smoked salmon, or a poached egg for a more substantial meal. The fritters can be made in advance and re-crisped in a 325°F oven when needed. They make good finger food for a lunch party—simply double or triple the recipe.

1 medium zucchini, shredded
1/3 cup low-fat ricotta cheese, drained
2 tbsp. buckwheat or whole-wheat flour
1 egg
1 garlic clove, minced

2 green onions, finely chopped
salt and black pepper
canola oil or low-fat cooking spray,
    to cook
lemon wedges, to serve

Put the shredded zucchini in a non-metallic sieve and press down to remove any excess liquid. Combine the ricotta, flour, and egg. Stir in the zucchini, garlic, and green onions, and season with salt and pepper.

Heat a griddle pan or large skillet and wipe with a paper towel that has been dipped in canola oil, or spray pan. Drop about 2 tablespoons batter onto the pan and spread out with the back of a spoon; repeat with the remaining batter. Cook for about 3 minutes on each side until crisp and golden. Remove from the pan and drain on paper towels. Serve hot, with lemon wedges.

Makes 2 servings

pesto & tomato soufflé

see variations page 86

Souffles are not difficult to cook and look really impressive when you serve them, but do be ready to eat them as soon as they appear out of the oven.

canola oil, to grease
2 tbsp. fine bread crumbs
2 tsp. low-fat butter or spread
2 tsp. flour

1/2 cup 1% milk
1/4 cup pesto (page 166)
2 eggs, separated
dash Tabasco sauce

2 egg whites
salt
6 cherry tomatoes, quartered
4 tsp. grated Parmesan cheese

Preheat oven to 350°F.

Prepare one 2-cup or two 1-cup soufflé dishes by brushing with canola oil in a vertical direction, which will help the soufflé to rise. Sprinkle with bread crumbs and tap out any excess.

In a small pan, melt the butter, stir in the flour, and cook for 1 minute. Slowly add milk and cook over a gentle heat, stirring constantly, until the mixture has thickened. Remove from heat. Stir in the pesto followed by the egg yolks and Tabasco sauce.

In a clean, dry bowl, beat the 4 egg whites with a pinch of salt until stiff peaks form. Stir one quarter of the egg whites into the pesto mixture to loosen it. Using a large metal spoon, fold in half the remaining egg whites. Fold in the quartered tomatoes, then the remaining egg whites.

Spoon the mixture into the prepared dishes and sprinkle with the Parmesan. Bake until well risen and brown, about 20 minutes for the small soufflés or 35 minutes for the larger one.

Makes 2 large or 3 small servings

mexican chicken wraps

see variations page 87

Packed full of fresh vegetables and chicken, these wraps are going to leave you satisfied. Look for low-carb tortillas; there are several varieties to choose from. These make a great way to painlessly drop the calorie count.

2 calorie-reduced tortillas
3/4 cup iceberg lettuce, shredded
2/3 cup cooked chicken, shredded
1/2 cup jicama or carrot, shredded

1/2 small red bell pepper, sliced
1 plum tomato, sliced
1/4 cup low-calorie medium or spicy salsa
1 tbsp. fresh cilantro, chopped

Lay out the tortillas and put half the lettuce down the center of each. Top with the chicken, jicama or carrot, bell pepper, and tomato. Drizzle the salsa down the middle and top with cilantro. Fold over both ends, then roll up tightly. Slice in half on the diagonal.

Makes 2 servings

cajun glazed mini chicken kebabs

see variations page 88

These spicy little kebabs are delicious at lunchtime broiled, as directed, or cooked over a grill. These go well with a pineapple salsa (page 47) and maybe a Cajun rice salad made from a little cooked rice and lots of mixed bell peppers, chopped jalapeño, celery, red onion, and fresh parsley. Alternatively serve with skewers of grilled vegetables or fruit.

marinade
2 tsp. Cajun spice mix
1 tbsp. light soy sauce
1 tsp. tomato paste
1 tbsp. lime juice
1 tbsp. pineapple juice from can

kebabs
1 large boneless, skinless chicken breast
4 pineapple chunks from can of pineapple in natural juice
4 (1-inch) chunks green bell pepper

Soak 4 small wooden skewers in water for 15 minutes.

Combine all the ingredients for the marinade in a bowl. Cut each chicken breast into 4 long slices lengthwise and then in half horizontally to give you 16 pieces. Toss into the marinade, making sure the chicken is evenly coated. Cover and let sit for at least 30 minutes.

Drain the chicken from the marinade and skewer chicken cubes onto soaked skewers, alternating with the pineapple and bell pepper. Broil kebabs on one side for 3 minutes. Turn and baste generously with remaining marinade and broil for a further 3 minutes, or until the chicken is thoroughly cooked through.

Makes 2 large or 4 small servings

open-faced sandwiches

see variations page 89

Otherwise known as smörgåsbord, this is the national dish of Denmark, where it is loved by everyone and often served as a do-it-yourself meal.

1/4 cup fat-free soft cream
   cheese
2 tbsp. low-calorie
   mayonnaise (page 20)
2 tbsp. fresh dill, chopped
1 tsp lemon juice
1 tsp. capers
salt and black pepper

4 pumpernickel or rye bread
   slices
4 small lettuce leaves
16 slices cucumber
1 hard-cooked egg, halved
   and sliced
3 oz. cooked shrimp
2 slices smoked salmon

to serve
1 tomato, quartered
2 dill pickles
fresh dill fronds and lemon
   wedges, to garnish

In a small bowl, combine the cream cheese, mayonnaise, dill, lemon juice, and capers. Season with salt and pepper.

Toast the bread, then spread slices with cheese mixture. Put a lettuce leaf on top and press down. Top with cucumber and egg. Then top 2 slices with cooked shrimp and 2 with salmon. Season with salt and pepper. Serve with tomato slices and dill pickles on the side and garnish with dill fronds and lemon wedges.

Makes 2 large or 4 small servings

variations

crustless quiche

see base recipe page 63

crusted mushroom quiche
Follow the basic recipe, replacing the zucchini shell with pastry (page 19).
Line the pastry with parchment paper and pie weights and bake at 375°F for
10 minutes. Remove the pie weights and paper and cook for a further
3 minutes to dry out base. Proceed as directed.

crustless leek & salmon quiche
Follow the basic recipe, omitting mushrooms, green onions, and thyme.
Cut 2 small leeks into slices and steam for 8 minutes until soft. Put on
the zucchini crust and top with 1 piece poached salmon, which has been
chopped, and 1 tablespoon chopped fresh dill. Proceed as for basic recipe.

crustless leek & ham quiche
Follow the recipe for leek and salmon quiche above, substituting 1 cup diced
smoked ham for the salmon and using chopped fresh parsley.

crustless spinach & feta quiche
Follow the basic recipe, omitting mushrooms and thyme. Steam 4 ounces
baby spinach leaves until just wilted, about 3 minutes, drain thoroughly,
then roughly chop. Put on the zucchini crust with the green onions and
1/2 cup crumbled feta cheese. Proceed as for basic recipe.

asparagus with poached egg

see base recipe page 64

garlic broccolini with poached egg
Follow the basic recipe, using steamed broccolini instead of asparagus. In a small skillet oiled with low-fat olive oil-flavored spray, gently cook 2 finely sliced garlic cloves until just golden. Sprinkle the broccolini with the garlic, and serve with the egg.

tomato with poached egg
Follow the basic recipe, using broiled tomato slices instead of asparagus. Slice 1 large beefsteak tomato into 1/4-inch slices and season with salt, pepper, and a pinch of sugar. Combine 2 tablespoons each dry bread crumbs, Parmesan cheese, and chopped fresh basil. Sprinkle over tomatoes. Broil for about 3 minutes until the topping is golden. Serve with the egg.

warm spinach salad with poached egg
Follow the basic recipe, using 8 ounces baby leaf spinach instead of asparagus. In a small skillet oiled with low-fat olive oil-flavored spray, gently cook spinach with 1 clove minced garlic and 1 finely chopped shallot. Once wilted, stir in 1 tablespoon balsamic vinegar, toss, and serve with the egg.

warm roasted vegetables with poached egg
Follow the basic recipe, using warm roasted vegetables (page 112) instead of asparagus.

variations

turkey & water chestnut lettuce wraps

see base recipe page 67

tofu & water chestnut lettuce wraps
Follow the basic recipe, using 6 ounces firm tofu instead of turkey. Press, drain, and crumble tofu into small pieces before stir-frying.

shrimp & water chestnut lettuce wraps
Follow the basic recipe, using 8 ounces raw small shrimp instead of turkey.

mexican chili lettuce wraps
Follow the basic recipe, seasoning the turkey with 1/2 teaspoon each chili powder, ground cumin, and hot paprika, and 1/4 teaspoon each ground coriander and dried oregano. Substitute 1/2 cup cooked corn for the water chestnuts, 1/4 cup salsa for the teriyaki sauce, and non-fat sour cream for the hoisin sauce.

indian lettuce wraps
Follow the basic recipe, seasoning the turkey with 1 tablespoon medium curry powder and using 1/2 cup cooked green lentils (canned are fine) instead of water chestnuts. Add 2 tablespoons raisins. Replace teriyaki sauce with 2 tablespoons soy sauce and 2 tablespoons water. Replace hoisin sauce with non-fat yogurt flavored with 2 tablespoons chopped mint, a squeeze of lemon, and a pinch of salt.

variations

minted feta parcels

see base recipe page 68

meaty parcels
Omit the spinach and feta. After the onion has softened, add 6 ounces extra-lean ground beef or turkey and 1 crushed garlic clove to the pan and brown all over. Add 1 chopped tomato, 1 tablespoon lemon juice, and 1 teaspoon tomato paste and cook for 5 minutes. Add the mint, nutmeg, salt, and pepper; cool and use to fill triangles as directed.

tomato feta parcels
Follow the basic recipe, adding 2 halved cherry tomatoes to each triangle.

dill & goat cheese parcels
Follow the basic recipe, using goat cheese instead of feta and dill instead of mint.

fennel & feta parcels
Follow the basic recipe, but omit mint. With the onion, cook 1/2 small fennel bulb, which has been chopped small (including fronds). When soft, add 1 peeled and chopped small tomato, and cook until the tomato juices evaporate. Cool and add to the spinach mixture and proceed as directed.

variations

garbanzo burgers with lemon tahini dressing

see base recipe page 69

garbanzo tuna burgers with lemon tahini dressing
Follow the basic recipe, using only 1/2 cup garbanzo beans and adding
1/2 (6-ounce) can tuna in water, drained.

black bean burgers with lemon tahini dressing
Follow the basic recipe, using black beans instead of garbanzo beans.

garbanzo burgers with tzatziki
Follow the basic recipe, replacing dressing with tzatziki sauce (page 54).

garbanzo burgers with peperonata
Follow the basic recipe, but serve with peperonata. Spray a skillet with
cooking oil and gently cook 1 chopped onion for 5 minutes. Add 1 minced
garlic clove, 2 sliced bell peppers, and 1/2 teaspoon crushed red pepper
flakes. Cook for 5 minutes. Add 1 (15-ounce) can crushed tomatoes. Bring to
a boil, then simmer for 5 minutes. Serve hot or at room temperature.

garbanzo burgers with mango relish
Follow the basic recipe, but serve with mango relish. Mix chopped flesh of 1
firm ripe mango, 1/4 cup chopped red onion, 1/2 seeded and chopped small
red chile, grated zest and juice of 1 lime, pinch of salt, and 1 tablespoon
chopped fresh cilantro.

zucchini & ricotta fritters

see base recipe page 70

vegan zucchini fritters
Follow the basic recipe, replacing the ricotta with 1/3 cup silken tofu. This works with all but the feta variation.

spicy zucchini ricotta fritters
Follow the basic recipe, adding 1 sliced jalapeño pepper, 1 tablespoon chopped fresh cilantro, and 1/2 teaspoon cayenne pepper with the zucchini.

corn ricotta fritters
Follow the basic recipe, omitting zucchini. Use instead 1 cup cooked corn kernels, 1/4 cup finely chopped red bell pepper, and 1/2 teaspoon dried red pepper flakes.

leftover vegetable ricotta fritters
Follow the basic recipe, omitting zucchini. Roughly grate or chop 1 cup leftover vegetables such as carrots, potatoes, or broccoli. Use along with 1 tablespoon chopped fresh parsley.

zucchini, ricotta & feta fritters
Follow the basic recipe, adding 1/2 cup crumbled feta with the zucchini.

variations

pesto & tomato soufflé

see base recipe page 73

pesto & ham soufflé
Follow the basic recipe, adding 2 ounces air-dried ham (visible fat removed)
to the mixture with the pesto.

pesto & sun-dried tomato soufflé
Follow the basic recipe, adding 3 tablespoons chopped sun-dried tomatoes
with the pesto. Omit cherry tomatoes.

goat cheese & herb soufflé
Follow the basic recipe, omitting pesto. Add 1/2 cup crumbled goat cheese
and 1 tablespoon each of chopped fresh parsley, basil, and chives.

butternut squash soufflé
Omit the flour and butter roux base and the pesto. Instead mix 2 cups
cooked, mashed butternut squash with the egg yolks, 1/2 teaspoon dried
sage, and 1/4 teaspoon mixed spice. Proceed as directed.

mexican chicken wraps

see base recipe page 74

curried chicken wraps
Follow the basic recipe, using carrot not jicama. Replace salsa with a mixture of 1/4 cup non-fat Greek yogurt, 1/2 teaspoon curry powder, 1 very finely chopped dried apricot, and 1/2 cup finely diced apple.

greek chicken wraps
Follow the basic recipe, using carrot not jicama. Replace salsa with a mixture of 1/4 cup non-fat Greek yogurt, 1/4 cup finely chopped cucumber, and 1/2 teaspoon lemon juice.

french chicken wraps
Follow the basic recipe, omitting cilantro and using shredded celeriac instead of carrot or jicama. Replace salsa with a mixture of 1/4 cup low-fat mayonnaise; 1 chopped green onion; 1/2 teaspoon each capers, Dijon mustard, and lemon juice; and 1 tablespoon chopped fresh tarragon.

italian chicken tuna wraps
Follow the basic recipe, omitting cilantro and using carrot not jicama. Replace salsa with a mixture of 1/4 cup low-fat mayonnaise; 1/4 cup canned tuna, drained and flaked; 1 mashed anchovy; 1 chopped green onion; and 1/2 teaspoon each capers, Dijon mustard, and lemon juice.

variations

cajun glazed mini chicken kebabs

see base recipe page 76

curried yogurt kebabs
Follow the basic recipe, replacing the marinade with mixture of 1/2 cup yogurt; 2 tablespoons lime juice; 1/2 teaspoon each cumin, grated fresh ginger, minced garlic, and paprika; and salt and pepper.

cajun glazed shrimp kebabs
Follow the basic recipe, substituting 16 small raw shrimp for the chicken. Broil or grill for 2–3 minutes on each side or until pink and cooked through.

cajun glazed beef kebabs
Follow the basic recipe, substituting 6 ounces lean beef (sirloin or top round) for the chicken. Omit pineapple and juice and increase lime juice to 2 tablespoons. Add 4 cherry tomatoes to the skewers. Broil or grill for 2 minutes on each side until beef is barely pink.

orange teriyaki glazed chicken kebabs
Follow the basic recipe, replacing the marinade with mixture of 1/4 cup teriyaki sauce, 2 tablespoons sugar-free orange marmalade, 1 tablespoon orange juice, and 1/4 teaspoon each powdered ginger and crushed red pepper flakes.

variations

open-faced sandwiches

see base recipe page 78

beef & grainy mustard open-faced sandwich

Follow the basic recipe, substituting 4 small slices lean cooked beef for the shrimp and salmon. Spread with a grainy honey mustard (or horseradish) and slice into strips. Use tomato slices instead of cucumber slices.

pickled herring open-faced sandwich

Follow the basic recipe, using 4 pickled herrings instead of shrimp or salmon. Use watercress instead of lettuce and add a few beet slices with the eggs.

hummus, carrot & red pepper open-faced sandwich

Put a layer of baby spinach leaves on top of each slice of bread. Spread 1–2 tablespoons low-fat hummus on top and then a few slices of fresh or jarred red bell pepper and shredded carrot. Sprinkle with a little lemon juice.

ham & fig open-faced sandwich

Spread the bread with fat-free cream cheese as in the basic recipe, omit other ingredients. Top each sandwich with a little watercress and then with 2 small slices of prosciutto; season with black pepper. Cut 2 fresh, ripe figs into 6 wedges and lightly brush with pomegranate molasses or balsamic vinegar. Put fig wedges on top of the ham.

soups

Soup makes a great low-calorie meal. What's more, everybody loves it. A bowl of blended soup has been proven to keep you fuller for longer than eating the same foods whole on a plate with a glass of water. A bowl of soup is stuffed full of vitamins and fiber, too! You'll have no trouble converting your family to become vegetable lovers with the tasty recipes in this chapter.

spicy butternut soup

see variations page 102

The rustic tastes and the rich color of fall are perfectly captured in this thick, spicy soup –
one to warm the cockles of your heart.

1/2 tbsp. canola oil or low-fat cooking spray
1 butternut squash (about 1 1/2 lbs.), peeled
    and cut into chunks
1 onion, chopped
1 garlic clove, minced
1–2 red chiles, seeded and finely chopped
1 tsp. ground cumin

3 1/2 cups low-sodium vegetable or chicken
    broth
1 bay leaf
4 tbsp. non-fat sour cream
salt and black pepper
fresh cilantro, chopped, to garnish

Heat the oil or cooking spray in a large saucepan, then add the squash and onion. Cook
gently for about 5 minutes until the onions have softened, stirring occasionally. Add the
garlic and chile to taste and cook for another 2 minutes, then add the ground cumin and
cook for a further minute.

Pour in the broth and bay leaf, increase the heat, and bring to a boil. Cover and simmer over
low heat for 15 minutes or until the squash is soft. Remove the bay leaf. Using an immersion
blender or a food processor, purée until smooth. Stir in half of the sour cream and season
with salt and pepper. Reheat, if necessary, and serve with a swirl of sour cream and some
chopped cilantro.

Makes 4 servings

zucchini & pea soup with lemon oil

see variations page 103

This summer soup is equally delicious served hot, at room temperature, or chilled. The lemon oil adds an extra flavor dimension, but may be omitted to cut calories.

2 tbsp. canola oil (or low-fat cooking spray
    and 1 1/2 tbsp. canola oil)
2 onions, chopped
2 stalks celery, chopped
3 medium zucchini, thickly sliced
1 1/2 cups shelled peas (fresh or frozen)
2 garlic cloves, minced

salt and black pepper
grated zest and juice of 1 lemon
1/2 cup fresh parsley, chopped
3 1/2 cups low-sodium vegetable or
    chicken broth
a little honey, to taste

Heat 1/2 tbsp. oil or spray in a large saucepan, then add the onions and celery. Cook gently for about 5 minutes until softened, stirring occasionally. Add the zucchini, peas, garlic, and some black pepper, and cook for 5 minutes. Stir in half of the lemon zest and juice, half of the parsley, and all of the broth. Bring to a boil; simmer for 15 minutes or until the vegetables are soft.

Meanwhile, make the lemon oil by combining the remaining lemon zest and juice with the remaining canola oil. Add a little salt and honey, to taste. Set lemon oil aside.

Using an immersion blender or a food processor, purée soup until smooth. Season with salt and pepper. Stir in the remaining parsley and serve drizzled with the lemon oil.

Makes 4–6 servings

old-fashioned chicken & barley soup

see variations page 104

This soup is possibly the best comfort food in the world, particularly if someone in the home is feeling a bit below par. You need only about half of the chicken, so strip off the rest and use in a salad.

1 broiler chicken (about
    2 lbs.), quartered, skin
    removed
2 onions, chopped
3 carrots, chopped

3 celery stalks, sliced
1 leek, sliced
8 cups water
1/2 cup pearl barley
2 bay leaves

1 tsp. dried sage
1/2 cup fresh parsley, chopped
salt and black pepper
1 tsp. chicken bouillon
    granules (optional)

Put the chicken and vegetables in a stockpot or very large saucepan, cover with the water, and add the pearl barley, bay leaves, sage, half of the parsley, and salt and pepper to taste. Bring to a boil, then simmer over low heat for 45 minutes, until the chicken is tender.

Remove the chicken from the pan, allow to cool, then strip the flesh off 2 quarters and shred. Reserve the other pieces for another meal. Discard the bay leaves and skim off any visible fat from the top of the broth. Return the meat to the pot, adding more chicken bouillon granules, if required to boost the chicken flavor of the broth. Adjust seasoning and reheat. Serve sprinkled with remaining parsley.

Makes 6 servings

mushroom & chestnut soup

see variations page 105

A lovely, rich, satisfying soup that belies its lightness and makes a perfect quick lunch. Portobello mushrooms are used for their deep flavor. Cremini mushrooms would work fine too, and wild mushrooms would be even more wonderful for a special occasion.

1 tbsp. low-fat spread
1 onion, chopped
1 garlic clove, minced
4 large portobello mushrooms, chopped
3 1/2 cups chicken or vegetable broth

1 (15-oz.) jar cooked peeled chestnuts,
    roughly chopped
1 tsp. dried thyme
salt and black pepper
fresh parsley, chopped, to garnish

Heat the spread in a large saucepan, then add the onion. Cook gently for about 5 minutes until the onion has softened, stirring occasionally. Add the garlic and cook for another 2 minutes, then stir in the mushrooms and continue cooking for about 8 minutes, stirring occasionally, until they have created their own liquid.

Add the chestnuts, broth, and thyme, then season with salt and pepper. Bring to a boil, then cover and simmer over low heat for 5 minutes. Using an immersion blender or a food processor, purée until smooth. Reheat if necessary and adjust the seasoning. Serve garnished with chopped parsley.

Makes 4 servings

gingered beet & carrot soup

see variations page 106

The rich color of this soup is magical and the taste sparkles to match. You might want to put on a pair of gloves when preparing the beets to avoid cerise pink fingers. Don't be temped to garnish with yogurt or sour cream, or the delicate flavors of this soup will be overpowered.

1/2 tbsp. canola oil or low-fat cooking spray
1 onion, chopped
2 tsp. fresh ginger, shredded
3 medium beets, chopped
3 medium carrots, chopped
4 cups low-sodium vegetable or chicken broth

2 bay leaves
grated zest of 1/2 orange
1/4 tsp. white pepper
salt
snipped chives, to garnish

Heat the oil or spray in a large saucepan, then add the onion. Cook gently for about 5 minutes until softened, stirring occasionally, then add the ginger and cook for 1 minute. Add the beets, carrots, broth, bay leaves, orange zest, white pepper, and salt. Bring to a boil, then cover and simmer over a low heat for 30 minutes or until the vegetables are soft.

Remove the bay leaves. Using an immersion blender or a food processor, purée until about half of the soup is smooth. Reheat the soup and serve garnished with snipped chives.

Makes 4 servings

fragrant shrimp soup

see variations page 107

This Thai soup marries the aromatic flavors of lemongrass, ginger, and lime and floods them through your kitchen.

1 tsp. canola oil or low-fat cooking spray
1 garlic clove, minced
3 cups low-sodium chicken broth
1 tbsp. soy sauce
2 tsp. fish sauce
2 medium carrots, thinly sliced
1 stalk celery, thinly sliced on the diagonal
4 cremini mushrooms, sliced

1 cup bok choy, shredded
1 stalk lemongrass
1 tsp. fresh ginger, minced
1–2 Thai red chile peppers, to taste
1/2 tsp. palm sugar or brown sugar
8 oz. raw small shrimp
2 tsp. lime juice
2 tbsp. basil leaves, sliced

Heat the oil in a large saucepan, tipping it slightly so that it pools in one area. Add the garlic and cook gently for a couple of minutes until soft and fragrant; do not brown. Add the broth, soy and fish sauces, vegetables, lemongrass, ginger, chiles, and sugar.

Bring the soup to a boil, cover, and simmer over low heat until the vegetables are tender, about 12 minutes. Stir in the shrimp, lime juice, and basil, and simmer for a few minutes until the shrimp have turned pink. Taste and adjust the quantities of soy and fish sauce, lime juice, and sugar as needed. Remove lemongrass before serving.

Makes 4–5 servings

simple curried lentil soup

see variations page 108

This is a main course soup that never fails to please. It couldn't be simpler to cook. This soup is fabulous textured or smooth, so take your pick. For a milder flavor, use cumin in place of the curry powder.

4 cups low-sodium chicken or vegetable broth
1 cup red lentils, rinsed
1 onion, chopped
2 garlic cloves, minced
1 large carrot, chopped
1 parsnip, chopped

2 tsp. curry powder
1/4 cup tomato paste
salt and black pepper
juice of 1/4 lemon
fresh cilantro, chopped, to garnish

In a large saucepan, put the broth, lentils, onion, garlic, carrot, parsnip, curry powder, and tomato paste. Bring to a boil, cover, and simmer over low heat for 20 minutes, until the lentils are tender. Season to taste.

For a smooth soup, purée, using an immersion blender or food processor and reheat.

Stir in the lemon juice and serve with chopped cilantro.

Makes 4–6 servings

minestrone alla milanese

see variations page 109

In Italy every *nonna* has her own recipe, and every district has its own version of this soup using local delicacies. The Milanese soup here uses rice and this recipe is the *crudo* version that doesn't precook the vegetables in oil, thus reducing the fat content.

1 onion, chopped
2 carrots, sliced
1 celery stalk, sliced
1 medium potato, chopped
2 oz. green beans, cut into 1-inch pieces
1 tbsp. fresh parsley, chopped (or 1 tsp. dried)
3 canned Italian plum tomatoes, chopped,
    plus 1/4 cup of their juices
4 cups low-sodium broth (chicken, beef, or
    vegetable)

1 medium zucchini, halved and cut into slices
4 oz. baby spinach leaves
1 cup green cabbage, shredded
salt and black pepper
1/4 cup risotto (Arborio) rice
2 tbsp. fresh basil, chopped
freshly grated Parmesan, or nutritional yeast,
    to serve

In a large saucepan, combine onion, carrots, celery, potato, green beans, parsley, tomatoes and juice, and broth. Season with salt and pepper. Bring to a boil, cover with the lid askew, and simmer over low heat for about 20 minutes. Add the rice and cook for 15–20 minutes, or until the vegetables are very tender and the rice cooked.

Add the zucchini, spinach, and cabbage, and cook for a further 8 minutes until these vegetables are very soft. Adjust the seasoning and stir in the basil. Serve the soup with freshly ground pepper and freshly grated Parmesan or, to reduce the calories, a sprinkling of nutritional yeast.

Makes 4–6 servings

variations

spicy butternut squash soup

see base recipe page 91

simple butternut squash soup
Follow the basic recipe, omitting the chiles and cumin. Add 2 long strips of lemon zest with the bay leaf; remove before serving. Add 1/4 teaspoon freshly ground nutmeg, or to taste, when stirring in the sour cream. Serve garnished with snipped chives instead of cilantro.

butternut squash & coconut soup
Follow the basic recipe, but reduce the broth to 2 1/2 cups. Add 1 cup low-fat coconut milk instead of sour cream, and heat through without boiling. Serve without sour cream garnish.

curried butternut squash soup
Follow the basic recipe, replacing the chiles and cumin with 1 1/2 teaspoons curry powder and the sour cream with non-fat yogurt. Alternatively, add the curry seasoning to the instructions for butternut squash and coconut soup above.

butternut squash & red bell pepper soup
Follow the basic recipe, adding 2 small red bell peppers, roughly chopped, with the squash. Substitute 1–2 tablespoons smoked paprika for the chiles and cumin. Omit the sour cream and serve garnished with parsley instead of cilantro.

zucchini & pea soup with lemon oil

see base recipe page 92

zucchini, pea & pesto soup
Follow the basic recipe, omitting the garlic, lemon zest and juice, parsley, and lemon oil garnish. Instead add 2 tablespoons pesto (page 166) just before blending the soup. Serve garnished with basil leaves.

leek, pea & ham soup
Follow the basic recipe, using the white parts of 3 medium leeks instead of the zucchini. After blending the soup with the parsley, add 1 cup chopped ham, visible fat removed, and 1/4 cup non-fat sour cream. Reheat to serve. Omit lemon oil.

chunky zucchini, pea & navy bean soup
Follow the basic recipe, but chop the zucchini into small chunks and omit the lemon oil garnish. Blend only one third of the soup and return to the pan. Add 1 (15-ounce) can navy beans to the soup and heat through before serving hot.

chilled zucchini, pea & mint soup
Follow the basic recipe, using 1/2 cup mint leaves instead of parsley. Serve with or without the lemon oil. This version is particularly good cold.

variations

old-fashioned chicken & barley soup

see base recipe page 94

cock-a-leekie

Follow the basic recipe, using just 1 onion and 2 leeks. Add 8 sliced prunes
to the broth when returning the chicken meat.

chicken noodle soup with pesto

Follow the basic recipe, omitting the sage and parsley. Add 2 tablespoons
basil pesto to the broth when returning the chicken meat.

reduced-fat cream of chicken soup

After the chicken is cooked through, strain the soup into another saucepan.
Discard solids. In a small pan, combine 1 cup fat-free evaporated milk,
1 1/2 tablespoons canola oil, and 1/3 cup sifted flour. Slowly bring to a boil,
stirring constantly. When thickened, gradually stir into the reserved broth,
then add the shredded chicken.

chicken soup with creole spices & tomato

Follow the basic recipe, but rub the chicken generously with creole seasoning
before cooking. Add 1 (15-ounce) can crushed tomatoes with the vegetables
and substitute brown basmati rice for the barley. Add more creole seasoning,
as needed, when returning the chicken to the pot.

variations

mushroom & chestnut soup

see base recipe page 95

creamy mushroom & chestnut soup
Follow the basic recipe, using 3 cups broth. Add 1 cup low-fat ricotta cheese to the soup when blending. Reheat without boiling before serving.

mushroom & leek soup
Follow the basic recipe, omitting the chestnuts. Cook 2 sliced medium leeks with the onions and increase the simmering time to 15 minutes to allow the leeks to soften.

mushroom & madeira soup
Follow the basic recipe, omitting the chestnuts and using 8 portobello mushrooms. Pour 1 tablespoon Madeira wine into the bottom of each bowl before serving.

mushroom, chestnut & quinoa soup
Follow the basic recipe, but while cooking the onions, toast 1/2 cup quinoa in a dry, heavy frying pan over medium heat until fragrant. Add the quinoa to the soup with the broth.

variations

gingered beet & carrot soup

see base recipe page 97

borscht
Follow the basic recipe, using 4 beets and 1 medium potato instead of the
carrots, and 1 minced garlic clove instead of the ginger. Omit orange zest
but add 2 tablespoons lemon juice. Serve with a swirl of non-fat sour cream.

beef & beet stew
Follow the instructions for borscht above, but add 8 ounces sliced steak that
has been tossed in lightly seasoned flour to the pan to cook with the onion.
Cook for a couple of minutes until browned on both sides, then continue as
instructed, using beef broth. Do not blend this main course soup.

carrot, coriander & orange soup
Follow the basic recipe, using 5 carrots and 1 medium potato instead of the
beets. Add 2 teaspoons ground coriander and a pinch of cinnamon in place
of the ginger, and use the zest and juice of the orange. This soup is best fully
blended and served with a swirl of non-fat yogurt and fresh cilantro.

curried carrot & yam soup with shredded kale
Follow the instructions for carrot & coriander soup above, using a small yam
instead of the potato. Use 2 teaspoons curry powder instead of cilantro and
cinnamon. Omit orange. Garnish with lightly steamed, finely shredded kale.

variations

fragrant shrimp soup

see base recipe page 98

fragrant shrimp & noodle soup
Prepare the basic recipe. Cook 4 ounces Thai rice noodles in a separate pan, following the package directions. Divide between the serving bowls and top with the soup.

fragrant thai vegetable soup
Follow the basic recipe, omitting the shrimp. With the vegetables, add 8 baby corn cobs, halved horizontally, and 1/2 cup canned bamboo shoots. If desired, add 1 cup tofu cubes.

fragrant coconut & shrimp soup
Follow the basic recipe, using only 2 cups broth. Add 1 cup low-fat coconut milk.

fragrant chicken soup
Follow the basic recipe, using 1 cup shredded chicken in place of shrimp. Simmer until the chicken is heated through.

variations

simple curried lentil soup

see base recipe page 99

simple curried green lentil soup
Follow the basic recipe, using green or Puy lentils in place of red lentils. Increase the cooking time to 35 minutes.

minted red lentil soup
Follow the basic recipe, using 1 teaspoon paprika and 1 teaspoon ground coriander instead of the curry powder. Add 1/4 cup chopped fresh mint with the lemon juice.

curried coconut & lentil soup
Follow the basic recipe, using 2 1/2 cups broth and adding 1 (15-ounce) can low-fat coconut milk.

red pepper & lentil soup
Follow the basil recipe, substituting 1 teaspoon smoked paprika (or cayenne pepper) if desired and 1 teaspoon ground cumin for the curry powder. Omit the parsnip and add 1 (12-ounce) jar roasted red peppers, drained and chopped (about 1 cup).

variations

minestrone alla milanese

see base recipe page 100

minestrone col il soffritto
Use the basic recipe ingredients, but begin with 2 tablespoons olive oil in a large pan. Add the onions and cook over low heat for 5 minutes, then add each of the vegetables in order (except tomatoes), cooking each for 2 minutes before adding the next. Once all the vegetables are added, stir in the tomatoes and juice, parsley, broth, and seasoning. Bring to a boil, cover, and simmer for 30 minutes.

ligurian minestrone
Follow the basic recipe, adding 3 tablespoons red pesto to the finished soup.

minestrone alla calabrese
Follow the basic recipe, but add 2 slices lean country ham or salt pork, chopped with fat removed, with the vegetables. Also add 1/2 cup each chopped red and yellow bell pepper with the cabbage.

minestrone pomodoro
Follow the basic recipe, reducing the broth to 3 cups and adding 1 cup tomato sauce with the broth.

salads

A good salad can feel like a treat rather than a penalty if the ingredients are delicious. It is essential that the raw ingredients are the very best you can find, so raiding the farmers' market or buying organic ingredients is highly recommended for intensity of flavor. The best salads are crisp and chilled, so be sure to store yours in the refrigerator until the last minute.

warm steak salad with earl grey vinaigrette

see variations page 124

Choose lean steak for this lovely, hearty salad. The use of Earl Grey tea in the dressing reduces the amount of oil while imparting a deliciously fragrant flavor to the dressing.

salad
- 4 cups mixed salad leaves, mesclun, or arugula
- 1/2 cup button mushrooms, sliced
- 4 tomatoes, chopped
- 1 red bell pepper, sliced
- 4 green onions, sliced
- 6 radishes, sliced

vinaigrette
- 1/4 tsp. garlic paste
- 2 tbsp. extra-virgin olive oil
- 2 tbsp. cold strong Earl Grey tea
- 2 tbsp. cider vinegar
- 1 tsp. Dijon mustard
- salt and black pepper

12 oz. rump steak, fat trimmed
cracked black pepper

Preheat broiler or grill. Distribute the salad ingredients between 4 dinner plates.

Put all the ingredients for the vinaigrette in a lidded jar and shake vigorously to combine.

Sprinkle the steak with cracked pepper. Put under the broiler or on the grill 3 inches away from the heat source and cook for 1 1/2–3 minutes on each side, until rare or medium, as liked. Let rest for 5 minutes in a warm place. Slice the steak thinly, arrange slices on top of the salad, and drizzle with the dressing.

Makes 4 servings

roasted vegetable salad

see variations page 125

This is a rich and healthful vegetarian salad. It also goes well with simple grilled fish, meat, or chicken; or vegetarians might like to add slices of grilled halloumi cheese.

1 fennel bulb, chopped
2 medium zucchini, chopped
8 oz. cherry tomatoes
1 small red bell pepper, thickly sliced
1 small yellow bell pepper, thickly sliced
2 red onions, cut into wedges
1 tbsp. fresh thyme, chopped
salt and pepper

2 tbsp. canola or olive oil or olive oil-flavored
  cooking spray
2 tbsp. balsamic vinegar
1 cup whole-grain couscous
1 1/2 cups boiling vegetable broth
2 cups mixed salad leaves
fresh basil leaves, to garnish

Preheat the oven to 425°F. Arrange the vegetables in a baking dish without overcrowding. Sprinkle with the thyme, salt, and pepper, then toss lightly with the oil, coating the vegetables evenly. Roast until the vegetables are tender and browned, turning halfway through cooking time. When cooked, drizzle with the balsamic vinegar and turn out onto a plate to cool.

Meanwhile, put the couscous in a heatproof bowl and stir in the boiling broth. Season with a pinch of salt, then stir with a fork. Cover with a dish towel and let stand for 5 minutes. The liquid should now be absorbed. Fluff with a fork; cool.

To assemble, put the lettuce on a plate, top with the couscous, and pile the roasted vegetables on top. Sprinkle with a few basil leaves to garnish.

Makes 4 servings

watercress, sesame & turkey salad with tangerine dressing

see variations page 126

This is a great recipe for using leftover roast turkey, but it works equally well with store-bought sliced turkey.

dressing
1 tbsp. tangerine zest
1/2 cup fresh tangerine
   juice
1 tbsp. canola oil
1 tsp. green onion, minced
1 tsp. fresh ginger, minced

1 tbsp. cider vinegar
pinch salt and black pepper

salad
2 tbsp. sesame seeds
2 bunches watercress,
   trimmed

8 radishes, quartered
2 celery stalks, sliced
1 carrot, cut into thin strips
1 apple, sliced
1 tbsp. lemon juice
4 thick slices turkey, chopped
2 tbsp. fresh chives, chopped

For the dressing, put all the remaining ingredients in a small jar and shake to mix.

For the salad, in a small skillet, dry-roast the sesame seeds until they just turn golden. Tip out and set aside to cool. Arrange the watercress on a platter, then scatter the radishes, celery, and carrots on top. Dip the apple slices in lemon juice to prevent discoloration, and add to the salad. Scatter the sesame seeds evenly over the salad. Pile the turkey into the center of the salad and top with the chives. Drizzle with the dressing.

Makes 4 servings

mixed leaf salad with creamy herb dressing

see variations page 127

This is the classic side dish suitable to eat with almost any main dish. The creamy herb dressing is vibrant and fresh and contains only about 10 calories per tablespoon. Double the quantities of salad greens, wash, and keep refrigerated in a resealable bag for another meal. This is less expensive than prepackaged salads and you know that it has been washed properly too. The variations later in this chapter have some other delicious salad dressing options.

1/2 small head radicchio	dressing	2 tbsp. fresh parsley, chopped
1/2 medium head Boston lettuce	3/4 cup low-fat buttermilk	1 tbsp. lemon juice
2 cups arugula	1/4 cup low-fat mayonnaise	2 tsp. Dijon mustard
1 cup pea shoots	1/4 cup green onions, snipped	salt and black pepper
	3 tbsp. fresh dill, chopped	

Arrange the salad greens in a bowl.

For the dressing, combine all the ingredients in a blender or lidded jar. Blend or shake until really smooth. Taste and adjust seasoning. (The dressing may be kept in a sealed container for up to 4 days in the refrigerator.)

Pour in enough dressing just to coat the greens, lightly toss, and serve immediately.

Makes 4 servings

asian shrimp rice noodle salad

see variations page 128

This is a delicious main course salad full of intense flavors and textures — a salad that is guaranteed to become a family favorite.

dressing
1 garlic clove, minced
1–2 long red chiles, seeded and finely
   sliced
1 tbsp. fresh ginger, minced
2 tbsp. fish sauce
1/3 cup lime juice
1 tbsp. brown sugar or equivalent in sugar
   substitute
1 tsp. sesame oil

salad
8 oz. small cooked shrimp
4 large cooked crayfish or large cooked shrimp
6 oz. cellophane or thin rice noodles
1/2 tbsp. canola oil or low-fat cooking spray
1 cup spinach, shredded
4 oz. sugar snap peas
1 cup bean sprouts
1/2 red bell pepper, sliced
1/4 cup fresh basil, chopped
1/4 cup fresh mint, chopped

For the dressing, combine all the ingredients in a lidded jar. Shake vigorously to combine. Pour over the cooked shrimp and crayfish. Let sit while the noodles are prepared.

Bring a large saucepan of water to a boil. Add the noodles, stir to separate, then cook according to package directions. Drain, refresh in cold water, then drain again. Transfer the noodles to a serving bowl. Let cool.

Toss the remaining ingredients into the cooled noodles, then toss with the small shrimp and all of the dressing. Arrange the crayfish or large shrimp on top of the dish to serve.

Makes 4 servings

quinoa party salad

see variations page 129

Make this salad in bulk for parties or potluck suppers. It is quick and easy to make and elegant to look at. The slightly nutty flavor of the quinoa works well with the pumpkin seeds and contrasts with the crunchy sweetness of the pomegranate.

2 cups vegetable broth or
   lightly salted water
1 cup quinoa
6 green onions, chopped

3 celery stalks, sliced
1/3 cup pumpkin seeds,
   toasted
1/4 cup fresh chives, snipped

1/4 cup fresh mint, chopped
seeds of 1 pomegranate
juice of 1 lime
2 tbsp. canola oil

Bring the vegetable broth or water to a boil in a saucepan. Add the quinoa, reduce the heat, and simmer for about 15 minutes until the water is absorbed and the quinoa has popped. Let cool, then break up with a fork.

Transfer the quinoa to a serving bowl and add the green onions, celery, pumpkin seeds, chives, mint, and pomegranate seeds. Toss to mix. Whisk together the lime juice and oil. Drizzle over the salad and toss gently to mix.

Serve at room temperature.

Makes 4–6 servings

lentil & mozzarella salad

see variations page 130

This is a filling salad that travels well, making it an ideal choice for lunchboxes, especially as it is best served at room temperature and the flavors deepen with time.

1 cup Puy lentils
1 bay leaf *
1 sprig thyme*
1 sprig rosemary*
salt
1 tbsp. canola oil or low-fat cooking spray
1 large onion, sliced
1 green bell pepper, sliced
1 red bell pepper, sliced

1 yellow bell pepper, sliced
4 oz. low-fat mozzarella, torn into small pieces
2 tbsp. soy sauce
2 tbsp. Worcestershire sauce
black pepper
1/4 cup parsley, to garnish

*If you do not have the fresh herbs, use a bouquet garni instead

Wash and pick over the lentils. Put in a saucepan with the bay leaf, thyme, and rosemary and a large pinch of salt. Cover the lentils with plenty of cold water and bring to a boil. Reduce the heat and simmer for about 25 minutes or until tender. Drain and refresh under cold water. Remove the herbs.

Meanwhile, heat the oil or spray in a skillet, add the onion, and cook for about 5 minutes until softened, stirring occasionally. Add the peppers and cook until they are soft; cool.

Combine the lentils, pepper–onion mixture, and mozzarella, then toss with the soy sauce, Worcestershire sauce, salt, and plenty of black pepper. Garnish with the parsley.

Makes 4-6 servings

pink coleslaw

see variations page 131

This pretty salad is a far cry from the slimy versions found in the supermarket. Coleslaw takes a lot of shredding, so it is worth making in a food processor. It keeps for at least a week in the refrigerator in a sealed container, so double the recipe while the food processor is out. Use the mayonnaise recipe (page 20) for maximum freshness.

1/4 red cabbage, shredded
2 carrots, shredded
1 large sweet onion, shredded
1/2 green bell pepper, shredded
salt

dressing
1/4 cup low-fat mayonnaise
2 tbsp. non-fat sour cream
1 tbsp. Dijon or grainy mustard
1/2 tsp. lemon juice
1/4 tsp. white pepper

Lay all the vegetables out on a chopping board and sprinkle very lightly with salt. Cover with a dish towel and let sit for 1 hour. Using the towel, dab the vegetables dry of any liquid that has formed and squeeze the vegetables very gently. Put the vegetables in a serving bowl.

In a small bowl, combine the mayonnaise, sour cream, mustard, lemon juice, and white pepper. Toss dressing with vegetables gently to coat evenly. Adjust the seasoning and serve.

Makes 4 servings

variations

warm steak salad with earl grey vinaigrette

see base recipe page 111

warm duck & mango salad with earl grey vinaigrette
Follow the basic recipe, using 2 small duck breasts instead of steak. Broil
duck breasts skin-side up for 10 minutes until the skin is browning and has
yielded most of its fat; pour off fat. Turn duck over and broil on the flesh
side for 5–10 minutes, depending on how rare you like the meat. Let rest for
5 minutes, then remove the skin before slicing thin. Add 1 sliced mango to
the salad ingredients.

warm lamb salad with earl grey vinaigrette
Follow the basic recipe, using lamb loin, trimmed of fat, instead of steak.

warm salmon salad with earl grey vinaigrette
Follow the basic instructions, using 4 small salmon fillets instead of steak.
Brush lightly with canola oil and season with salt and pepper. Broil for
5–8 minutes on each side depending on thickness and personal taste.

prosciutto & peach salad with earl grey vinaigrette
Follow the basic recipe, using 3 slices prosciutto or other air-dried ham
instead of the steak. Tear ham into strips and arrange on the salad. Add
1/2 cup shaved Parmesan cheese and 1 sliced peach to the salad.

roasted vegetable salad

see base recipe page 112

hot roasted vegetables
Roast the vegetables as directed and serve hot as a side dish instead of as a salad.

roasted vegetable tartlets
Roast the vegetables as directed. Reduce oven temperature to 350°F. Take 4 sheets of phyllo pastry. Lay the first sheet on a piece of parchment paper, spray with a light film of olive oil, top with next sheet, spray, and repeat with remaining sheets. Cut the sheets into 24 squares. Put each square of stacked phyllo into a lightly oiled muffin cup and fill with the roasted vegetables. Bake for 5–7 minutes.

roasted vegetable omelet
Prepare the omelet as directed on page 28 and fill with 4 tablespoons of roasted vegetables instead of tomatoes. A good use for leftovers.

roasted root vegetable & feta cheese salad
Follow the basic recipe, replacing the vegetables with 1 bunch each of baby carrots and small beets, trimmed; 2 parsnips, cut into large chunks; and 2 red onions, cut into wedges. Bake until golden brown, about 45 minutes. Serve salad warm, dotted with 3 ounces crumbled feta cheese.

watercress, sesame & turkey salad with tangerine dressing

see base recipe page 114

watercress, sesame & tuna salad with tangerine dressing
Follow the basic recipe, using 2 cups canned or cooked fresh tuna chunks instead of the turkey.

watercress, sesame & turkey salad with goat cheese
Follow the basic recipe, scattering 6 ounces crumbled goat cheese over the salad.

asian turkey sesame salad
Follow the basic recipe, using pea shoots instead of watercress and omitting the apple. Add 1 1/2 cups bean sprouts and 1/2 cup sliced bamboo shoots to the salad. To the dressing, add 2 tablespoons soy or teriyaki sauce.

watercress, sesame & tofu salad
Follow the basic recipe, using 1 (12-ounce) package marinated light tofu in place of the turkey. The tofu variation works equally well with the Asian version above.

mixed leaf salad with creamy herb dressing

see base recipe page 115

mixed leaf salad with fresh tomato basil dressing
Prepare the basic salad. For the dressing, halve 2 medium ripe tomatoes, then grate the cut edges over a pitcher and discard skins. Stir in 1 tablespoon each red wine vinegar, olive oil, and chopped basil. Season with salt and pepper and stir in 1 tablespoon chopped fresh basil.

mixed leaf salad with poppy seed dressing
Prepare the basic salad. For the dressing, combine 1/2 cup low-fat sour cream, 1/2 cup non-fat yogurt, 2 tablespoons honey or sugar substitute, 2 tablespoon apple juice, and 2 teaspoons poppy seeds. Mix until really smooth.

mixed leaf salad with caesar dressing
Prepare the basic salad. For the dressing, combine 3/4 cup low-fat buttermilk, 1/4 teaspoon garlic paste, 1 mashed anchovy fillet, 1/2 cup shredded Parmesan cheese, and 2 teaspoons white wine vinegar. Season with salt and black pepper. Mix until really smooth.

mixed leaf salad with raspberry vinaigrette
Prepare the basic salad. For the dressing, combine 1/2 cup raspberry vinegar, 1/3 cup canola oil, 2 tablespoons honey or sugar substitute, 2 teaspoons Dijon mustard, and a pinch dried sage. Season with salt and black pepper and mix until really smooth.

variations

asian shrimp rice noodle salad

see base recipe page 117

asian noodle salad with roasted tofu

Follow the basic recipe, substituting soy sauce for the fish sauce and omitting the seafood. Slice 1 12-ounce package extra-firm tofu, which has been pressed and drained, cut into 3/4-inch cubes. Use the dressing as a marinade for the tofu and let sit for 1–4 hours, turning occasionally. Remove the tofu from the marinade, spread out on a baking sheet, reserving marinade. Roast tofu in a 450°F oven for about 20 minutes, until golden; let cool. Combine with the other ingredients as directed.

soba noodle seafood mango salad

Follow the basic recipe, using soba (buckwheat) noodles instead of rice noodles. Also replace the bean sprouts and sugar snap peas with 1 cup thin cucumber sticks and 1 sliced mango.

asian noodle salad with shredded chicken

Follow the basic recipe, using 2 cold cooked chicken breasts, cooled and shredded instead of the seafood. Do not marinate the chicken.

asian noodle salad with crabmeat

Follow the basic recipe, using 8 ounces cooked shredded crabmeat instead of the small shrimp.

variations

quinoa party salad

see base recipe page 118

mexican quinoa salad

Prepare the quinoa as directed. Omit the pomegranate. Add to cooled quinoa 1/2 cup each of chopped red and green bell pepper; 1–2 jalapeño chiles, seeded and finely chopped; and 1/2 cup corn kernels. Substitute cilantro for the mint. Add 1/2 teaspoon each of chili powder, cumin, and oregano to the dressing with salt and pepper to taste.

israeli couscous party salad

Follow the basic recipe, using 1 1/2 cups Israeli couscous instead of quinoa. Toast couscous in a hot heavy skillet for about 5 minutes, until golden. Add 2 cups water, bring to a boil, reduce the heat, and simmer for about 12 minutes until just tender and the water has evaporated.

turkish salad

Follow the basic instructions, but omit green onions, celery, and pomegranate and use pine nuts instead of pumpkin seeds. Add 2 medium chopped tomatoes, 1 cup chopped cucumber, 1/4 cup halved black olives, and 1 small chopped red onion. Season with salt and pepper.

main course quinoa salad

Make the basic salad or any of the salad variations. Add to the final dish 1 cup shredded cooked chicken, turkey, shrimp, or tuna, and 1/2 cup crumbled feta cheese.

variations

lentil & mozzarella salad

see base recipe page 121

lentil & mozzarella salad with roasted vegetables
Follow the basic recipe, omitting the soy and Worcestershire sauces. Roast a
selection of vegetables (page 112). Lay lentils on a platter, top with vegetables,
and sprinkle with mozzarella. Served at room temperature or warm.

moroccan spiced lentil salad
Follow the basic recipe, omitting the soy and Worcestershire sauces.
Instead make a dressing with 1/4 cup lemon juice, 2 teaspoons olive oil,
and 1 teaspoon each of ground cumin and red pepper flakes.

bulgur, pepper & mozzarella salad
Follow the basic recipe, using bulgur instead of lentils. Put 1 1/2 cups
medium bulgur in a large pot. Add 3 cups boiling water, stir, cover, and set
aside until the bulgur has softened, about 15 minutes. Put in a strainer and
press down to remove any excess liquid before proceeding.

lentil & soybean salad
Follow the basic recipe, omitting the onions, bell peppers, and mozzarella. To
the cooled lentils add 1 cup cooked soybeans or lima beans, 1 finely chopped
small red onion, 1 cup halved cherry tomatoes, 1 chopped red bell pepper,
1/2 cup chopped cucumber, and substitute lemon juice for the
Worcestershire sauce. Sprinkle with chopped fresh parsley to garnish.

variations

pink coleslaw

see base recipe page 122

marinated coleslaw
Put the shredded vegetables in a bowl. Combine 1 tablespoon canola oil,
3 tablespoons cider vinegar, 2 teaspoons dry mustard, 1/2 teaspoon salt, and
1/4 teaspoon white pepper. Toss over the vegetables and mix well. Cover and
set aside for 12–24 hours. Drain off as much of the marinade as possible and
discard. You may like your coleslaw just like this, but for a creamy coleslaw,
proceed as with basic recipe.

classic coleslaw with apple
Follow the basic recipe, using white cabbage instead of red cabbage.
Add 1 red-skinned apple such as Pink Lady, cut onto thin wedges, with
the dressing.

pink coleslaw with fennel & radishes
Follow the basic recipe, adding 1 shredded small fennel bulb and 1/4 cup
sliced radishes to the vegetables.

pink coleslaw with celeriac & walnuts
Follow the basic recipe, adding 1 cup shredded celeriac to the vegetables.
Toss 1/4 cup chopped walnuts over the finished salad.

slow-cooked main dishes

The great thing about this type of food is convenience. Most of the recipes are simple to put together, then you just pop them in the oven and forget about them. While you are getting on with your life, the flavors in the pot slowly meld together and take on a life of their own.

navy bean & sausage bake

see variations page 146

Navy beans are full of cholesterol-lowering fiber and are an almost fat-free protein.
So, if you go easy on the sausage, prebroil it, and remove the fat, this dish is ideal for a
calorie-restricted diet.

6 turkey sausages
1/2 tbsp. canola oil or
   low-fat cooking spray
1 onion, chopped
3 garlic cloves, minced
1 green bell pepper,
   sliced
2 leeks, sliced

2 carrots, chopped
1/2 parsnip, chopped
1 (15-oz.) can cherry
   tomatoes (or 8 oz. cherry
   tomatoes and 1/2 cup
   tomato sauce)
1 (15-oz.) can navy beans,
   rinsed and drained

1 1/2 cups low-sodium
   chicken broth
1 tbsp. paprika
1 tsp. dried thyme
1 tbsp. balsamic vinegar
1 tsp. Worcestershire sauce
salt and black pepper
8 oz. baby spinach

Preheat the broiler.

Broil the sausages about 4 inches from the heat source for 5 minutes, then turn with a pair
of tongs and cook another 5 minutes. Remove onto paper towels and dry off any visible fat;
slice when cool. Reduce the oven temperature to 350°F.

Meanwhile, heat the oil or spray in a Dutch oven, then add the onion. Cook gently for about
5 minutes until softened, stirring occasionally. Add the garlic and cook for 1 minute. Add the
sliced sausage and the remaining ingredients except for the spinach. Cook in the oven for 45
minutes. Add the spinach and stir until wilted (if cooking ahead of time, add the spinach
after reheating). Adjust the seasoning and serve.

Makes 4 servings

spanish chorizo chicken casserole

see variations page 147

The trick here is to use just enough chorizo to flavor the stew without compromising your fat intake. The recipe includes a few judicious potatoes, so simply serve with a green salad.

3 in. dried chorizo sausage, skinned and
    thinly sliced
4 skinless chicken thighs
salt and black pepper
1 red onion, chopped
4 garlic cloves, thinly sliced
1 red bell pepper, sliced
1 yellow bell pepper, sliced

1 medium zucchini, sliced
8 cremini mushrooms, quartered
1 (15-oz.) can chopped tomatoes
8 small potatoes, halved
1 1/2 cups low-sodium chicken broth
1 tsp. dried rosemary
2 tsp. paprika
3/4 tsp. crushed red pepper flakes

Preheat the oven to 350°F.

Set a Dutch oven over medium heat. Add the chorizo and cook, stirring, until the chorizo has rendered some of its fat and is beginning to brown. Remove from the pot and drain on paper towels. Season the chicken with salt and pepper. Drain off the rendered fat in the pot, leaving the residue. Add the chicken thighs, brown on both sides, then put on paper towels to drain.

Drain any excess fat from the pot and add the onion. Cook gently for about 5 minutes until softened, stirring occasionally. Add the garlic and cook for 1 minute. Return the chicken and chorizo to the pot and add all the remaining ingredients. Bring to a boil. Transfer to the oven and bake for 45 minutes or until the chicken and potatoes are cooked through.

Makes 4–5 servings

lamb & zucchini tagine

see variations page 148

Lamb isn't the leanest meat, so choose it wisely and cut off all the visible fat. Serve in the traditional way with steamed couscous.

1/2 tbsp. canola oil or low-fat cooking spray
1 lb. diced lean lamb
4 garlic cloves, sliced
1 tsp. ground cumin
1/2 tsp. ground cinnamon
1/2 tsp. ground ginger
1/2 tsp. chili powder

1 1/2 cups low-sodium beef broth
1 tbsp. tomato paste
1 tbsp. honey
1/2 cup dried apricots
salt to taste
2 zucchini, cut into chunks
chopped fresh cilantro and harissa, to garnish

Preheat the oven to 325°F.

Heat the oil or spray in a Dutch oven, then add the lamb and cook over medium-high heat, stirring often to evenly brown the meat. Remove from the pot. Add the onion to the pot and cook gently for about 5 minutes until softened, stirring occasionally. Add the garlic and cook for 1 minute. Add the spices and cook for 1 minute more.

Return the lamb to the pot, pour in the broth, and stir in the tomato paste, honey and apricots. Bring to a boil, cover the Dutch oven, and cook in the oven for 1 1/4 hours, stirring once every 15 minutes, and adding a little water or broth if necessary. Taste to adjust the seasoning and sweetness. Stir in the zucchini and cook for about 15 minutes until the zucchini is soft. Serve garnished generously with chopped cilantro and accompanied by harissa paste.

Makes 4 servings

meatballs in char-grilled pepper sauce

see variations page 149

Ground beef may still be high in fat, so look out for extra-lean ground steak instead.

meatballs
1/4 cup bulgur
8 oz. extra-lean ground
  steak
1 cup whole wheat bread
  crumbs
4 green onions, very finely
  chopped
1 garlic clove, minced

1 small egg white, lightly
  whisked
1 tsp. tomato paste
1 tbsp. balsamic vinegar
1 tbsp. fresh parsley, chopped
pinch ground cinnamon and
  nutmeg
salt and black pepper
1 tbsp. canola oil

red pepper sauce
5 roasted peppers from a jar
1/2 small red onion
2/3 cup water
1 tbsp. tomato paste
1 tsp. garlic paste
1/2–1 tsp. smoked paprika
2 tbsp. lemon juice
salt

Put the bulgur in a medium bowl and cover generously with hot water. Soak for 30 minutes, then drain in a fine sieve. Add the remaining ingredients to the bulgur and use your hands to combine. Add a little water if the mixture seems a bit dry. Roll the mixture into 12 meatballs.

Preheat oven to 350°F. Heat the oil in a large non-stick skillet. Add the meatballs and cook, turning occasionally, until evenly browned, about 5 minutes. Remove from the skillet with tongs and drain on paper towels. Put meatballs into Dutch oven.

Make the sauce by combining the peppers, onion, water, tomato paste, and garlic paste in a blender. Process to form a smooth sauce. Add the paprika, lemon juice, and a little salt, to taste. Pour sauce over the meatballs, cover, and bake in the oven for 40 minutes.
Makes 4 servings

turkey moussaka

see variations page 150

Using ground turkey, roasting the eggplant, and using a low-fat sauce cuts the calories.

2 tbsp. olive oil or olive oil-
  flavored cooking spray
1 onion, chopped
2 garlic cloves, minced
2 carrots, chopped
1 celery stalk, sliced
1 lb. ground turkey
1/2 tsp. ground cinnamon
generous grating nutmeg

1 (15-oz.) can chopped
  tomatoes
1/2 cup low-sodium chicken
  broth
2 tbsp. tomato paste
2 tsp. balsamic vinegar
1 tsp. dried oregano
1/4 cup fresh parsley, chopped

2 medium eggplants, sliced
  1/4-inch thick
salt and black pepper
juice 1/2 lemon

sauce
1 cup low-fat cream cheese
4 oz. feta cheese, crumbled
1 egg

Preheat oven to 425°F.

Heat the oil or spray in a large skillet, add the onion, and cook for about 5 minutes until softened, stirring occasionally. Add the garlic, carrots, and celery, and cook for 1 minute. Add the ground turkey and cook over high heat to brown the meat. Stir in the cinnamon and nutmeg, followed by the tomatoes, broth, tomato paste, vinegar, and oregano. Cover and simmer over low heat for 30 minutes. Stir in the parsley.

Meanwhile, lightly oil 2 large cookie sheets. Lay the eggplant slices on top, brush with a little oil, season with salt and pepper, and drizzle with lemon juice. Bake for about 20 minutes until golden brown. Reduce oven temperature to 350°F. Oil an 8x10-inch baking dish, add a layer of meat followed by a layer of eggplant; repeat. Combine cream cheese, feta, and eggs, and spread over the moussaka. Bake for 50–60 minutes until golden brown.

Makes 6 servings

big beef stew

see variations page 151

Slow-cooked beef and hearty vegetables make this the ultimate comfort dish to come home to on a cold winter's day. This recipe uses a low-fat cut of beef and cooks on a low temperature (be sure not to boil or the beef will toughen). Using balsamic vinegar to good effect has also ridded the dish of the empty calories in red wine. As potatoes are included, there is no need for a side dish other than some steamed fresh green vegetables.

1/2 tbsp. canola oil or low-fat cooking spray
1 lb. round roast, trimmed of fat
black pepper
paprika
1 large onion, chopped
2 garlic cloves, minced
2 tbsp. flour
3 tbsp. balsamic vinegar
2 1/2 cups low-sodium beef broth
2 medium carrots, chopped
1 large parsnip, chopped

2 celery stalks, sliced
1 large tomato, skinned, seeded, and chopped
3 medium red-skinned potatoes, chopped
2 tbsp. sun-dried tomato paste
2 bay leaves
1/2 tsp. dried thyme
pinch dried rosemary
salt
3/4 cup thickly sliced mushrooms
2 tbsp. fresh parsley, chopped

Heat the oil or spray in a Dutch oven. Season the beef with a little black pepper and paprika, then add in batches, taking care not to overcrowd the pot. Cook over high heat, stirring occasionally, until browned all over. Remove with a slotted spoon. Add the onion to the pot and cook gently for about 5 minutes until softened, stirring occasionally. Add the garlic and cook for 1 minute.

Sprinkle the flour over the cooked onion and garlic, and cook for a further minute, stirring constantly. Add the vinegar and cook for another minute, then slowly add one-third of the

beef broth, stirring hard to deglaze the bottom of the pot. Add the remaining broth. Return the meat to the pot with the remaining ingredients except the mushrooms and parsley. Increase the heat to medium-high and bring the stew to a simmer (when just a few bubbles are rising to the surface). Reduce the heat to low and simmer for 1 1/2 hours. Adjust the seasoning and add the mushrooms, simmer for 15 minutes, remove the bay leaves, and stir in the parsley.

Makes 4 servings

italian-style fish stew

see variations page 152

You can prepare the rich, aromatic sauce in advance, and then reheat it, adding the fish and saffron just 15 minutes before you serve.

1/2 tbsp. canola oil or low-fat cooking spray
1 large onion, chopped
3 garlic cloves, minced
1 celery stalk, sliced
1 green bell pepper, chopped
1 1/2 (15-oz.) cans tomatoes or 1 1/2 lb. fresh
   ripe tomatoes, peeled, seeded, and chopped
2 1/2 cups fish broth or 1 1/2 cups clam juice
   and 1 cup water

2 bay leaves
4 anchovy fillets, chopped
2 strips orange zest
salt and black pepper
1 lb. mild white fish such as cod or red snapper
8 oz. raw shrimp or squid
pinch saffron
4 black olives, sliced
2 tablespoons fresh basil, chopped

Heat the oil or spray in a large skillet, then add the onion. Cook gently for about 5 minutes until softened, stirring occasionally. Add the garlic, celery, and bell pepper, and cook gently for 5 minutes until just turning a golden color. Stir in the tomatoes, broth, and bay leaves, increase the heat, and bring to a boil. Reduce the heat to a simmer, then add the anchovies and orange zest. Season with salt and pepper. Allow to simmer gently for 15 minutes to form a rich tomato sauce.

Gently put the fish and shrimp or squid into the stew with the saffron. Simmer gently without boiling for 15 minutes. Remove the orange zest and bay leaves and stir in the black olives and basil to serve.

Makes 4 servings

black bean stew with eggs

see variations page 153

Beans and eggs are both great sources of protein, low in calories and inexpensive. Cooked with the warming flavors of the spices, this makes a wholesome and satisfying meal.

1/2 tbsp. canola oil or low-fat cooking spray
1 large onion, chopped
2 garlic cloves, finely chopped
1 carrot, chopped
1 fresh red chile, seeded and chopped
1 1/2 tsp. ground cumin
1/4 tsp. smoked paprika
2 bay leaves

2 (15-oz.) cans black beans, rinsed
1 1/2 cups low-sodium vegetable broth
1 cup chopped canned tomatoes
1 tsp. dried thyme
salt and black pepper
juice 1/2 lime
4 eggs
2 tbsp. fresh cilantro, chopped

Preheat oven to 350°F.

Heat the oil or spray in a large skillet, then add the onion. Cook gently for about 5 minutes until softened, stirring occasionally. Add the garlic, carrot, and chile, and cook for 1 minute. Add the cumin, paprika, and bay leaves, and cook for 2 minutes more.

Add the beans, broth, tomatoes, and thyme. Season to taste with salt and pepper. Increase the heat and bring to a boil. Pour into a shallow baking dish, cover, and cook for 30 minutes. Remove the bay leaves and stir in the lime juice. Make 4 wells in the stew and carefully break an egg into each. Return to the oven and bake, uncovered, for 10–14 minutes or until the egg whites are set and the yolk is done to your liking. Serve sprinkled with cilantro.

Makes 4 servings

variations

navy bean & sausage bake

see base recipe page 133

navy bean & ham bake

Follow the basic recipe, omitting sausages. With the vegetables, add 6 slices of smoked ham, trimmed of all visible fat.

quick navy bean & sausage bake

Follow the basic recipe, omitting leeks, carrot, and parsnip, and adding 1 (14-ounce) package mixed frozen vegetables. Bring to a boil and simmer on the stovetop for 15 minutes, before adding the spinach.

spicy black beans & sausage bake

Follow the basic recipe, using black beans instead of navy beans. With the garlic, add 2 teaspoons ground cumin and 1–3 chopped jalapeño chiles, to taste.

puy lentil & sausage bake

Follow the basic recipe, replacing beans with 3/4 cup Puy lentils that have been washed and picked over. Increase the broth to 3 cups. Bake for 25–30 minutes until the lentils are just cooked.

variations

spanish chorizo chicken casserole

see base recipe page 134

mexican chorizo chicken casserole
Follow the basic recipe, omitting rosemary, paprika, and red pepper flakes.
Use instead 1 teaspoon each of ground cumin and dried oregano, and 2
tablespoons chopped chipotle in adobo sauce.

chicken curry
Omit the chorizo, rosemary, and paprika. Rub the chicken with a spice mix
made from 1 teaspoon each of chili powder and black mustard seeds, and
1/2 teaspoon each of ground cinnamon, cumin, ginger, and turmeric. Let sit
in the refrigerator for 1 hour. Brown the chicken in 1/2 tablespoon canola oil
or low-fat spray and proceed with basic recipe. Serve with non-fat yogurt.

spanish chorizo seafood casserole
Follow the basic recipe, omitting chicken. Cook the remaining ingredients for
20 minutes, then remove from the oven and add 8 ounces raw shrimp and
12 ounces white fish fillets, cut into large chunks. Cook just 15–20 minutes,
until fish is cooked through. Serve with lemon wedges.

pork & chorizo casserole
Follow the basic recipe, replacing chicken thighs with 1 pound pork loin,
trimmed of fat and cut into 1-inch cubes. Reduce the oven temperature to
325°F and Increase the cooking time to 1 1/2 hours.

variations

lamb & zucchini tagine

see base recipe page 137

lamb tagine with preserved lemon & olives
Follow the basic recipe, omitting the apricots. With the broth add a well-rinsed preserved lemon, flesh removed, and sliced into wedges, and 1/3 cup green olives.

chicken tagine with squash
Follow the basic recipe, omitting the lamb and zucchini. Instead, use 4 skinless chicken thighs and 1 pound chopped butternut squash. Add the butternut squash with the broth and cook for 1 1/2 hours.

lamb tagine with prunes & pumpkin
Follow the basic recipe, omitting the apricots and zucchini. Instead, use 12 dried whole prunes, and add 1 pound chopped pumpkin with the broth.

garbanzo & green bean tagine
Follow the basic recipe, omitting the lamb and begin by cooking the onion in the oil. With the broth add 1 1/2 cups cooked or canned garbanzo beans and 4 carrots cut into 2-inch sticks. Add 8 ounces green beans instead of the zucchini. This variation also works well with prunes; see above.

variations

meatballs in char-grilled pepper sauce

see base recipe page 138

meatballs in italian sauce
Follow the basic meatball recipe. For the sauce, put in a saucepan
1 (28-ounce) can chopped tomatoes, 2 teaspoons garlic paste, 2 tablespoons
tomato paste, 1/4 cup basil pesto, and 1/2 teaspoon crushed red pepper
flakes. Bring to a boil and cook for 2 minutes. Proceed as directed.

meatballs in curry sauce
Follow the basic meatball recipe. For the sauce, put in a saucepan
1 (28-ounce) can chopped tomatoes, 2 tablespoons medium curry paste,
1 tablespoon lemon juice, 2 teaspoons garlic paste, and 1 teaspoon crushed
red pepper flakes. Bring to a boil and cook for 2 minutes. Proceed as directed.

greek meatballs
Follow the basic meatball recipe, replacing the parsley with chopped fresh
mint and adding 1 teaspoon lemon zest. Fry the meatballs, turning often,
until cooked through, about 15 minutes. Instead of cooking in the red
pepper sauce, serve with tzatziki, made by combining 3/4 cup non-fat yogurt;
1 3-inch piece cucumber, seeded and chopped; and 3 tablespoons chopped
fresh mint.

turkey meatballs in char-grilled pepper sauce
Follow the basic recipe, using ground turkey instead of ground steak.

variations

turkey moussaka

see base recipe page 139

vegetarian moussaka with lentils
Follow the basic recipe, substituting 2 cups cooked red or brown lentils for
the turkey and omitting the browning phase. Add the lentils and 1 bay leaf
with the tomatoes. Remove the bay leaf before baking.

moussaka with zucchini
Follow the basic recipe, substituting 3 large zucchini sliced lengthwise into
thick strips for the eggplant. Oven-roast as directed or, to reduce fat, blanch
in boiling water for 2 minutes before using.

stuffed bell peppers
Make the turkey filling; omit eggplant and cheese sauce. Halve 4 large red or
green bell peppers lengthwise and remove seeds and membranes, keeping the
shells intact. Stuff the cavities with turkey filling, then sprinkle with 2
tablespoons bread crumbs mixed with 2 tablespoons Parmesan cheese. Put
on a baking tray and bake, uncovered, for 30 minutes. This works well with
the vegetarian filling too.

beef moussaka
Follow the basic recipe, using extra-lean ground steak in place of turkey or
a combination of half steak and half TVP ground beef substitute.

variations

big beef stew

see base recipe page 140

big beef & barley stew
Follow the basic recipe. After the stew has been simmering for 1 1/4 hours, add 1 cup pearl barley, stir, and return to a simmer.

big pork stew with chiles
Follow the basic recipe, using pork loin instead of beef. With the garlic, add 1 teaspoon chili powder; 1 teaspoon cumin; 2 Anaheim chiles, seeded and chopped; and 1 seeded and sliced red bell pepper. Omit the parsnip. Add 1 large chopped zucchini for the last 15 minutes instead of the mushrooms.

big beef stew with cabbage
Follow the basic recipe, omitting the parsnip and potatoes and adding 1 tablespoon crushed red pepper flakes and 2 additional teaspoons paprika. Roughly chop 1 medium cabbage and add to the stew instead of the mushrooms, adding a little more hot water, if required.

big beef curry
Follow the basic recipe, but with the garlic add 1/2 teaspoon minced fresh ginger and 2 tablespoons medium curry powder. Omit rosemary and thyme and replace the parsley with chopped fresh cilantro. Serve with non-fat yogurt, if desired.

variations

Italian-style fish stew

see base recipe page 143

southern-style fish stew
Follow the basic recipe, adding 3/4 cup diced potato, 1/2 cup corn kernels,
1 teaspoon Worcestershire sauce, 1 dash Tabasco, and 1/4 teaspoon ground
cloves with the broth. Omit olives and replace basil with flat leaf parsley.

caribbean-style fish stew
Follow the basic recipe, adding 1 scotch bonnet or habañero pepper and
1/4 teaspoon dried thyme with the bell pepper and 1 teaspoon brown sugar
with the tomatoes. Omit the olives. Replace fresh basil with fresh cilantro
and add the juice of 1 lime to finish.

california-style fish stew
Follow the basic recipe, using 12 ounces Pacific fish (such as mahi-mahi or
Pacific halibut) and 6 ounces each of raw shrimp and sea scallops. Omit
olives and replace basil with flat leaf parsley.

north african fish stew
Follow the basic recipe, adding 1 teaspoon each ground cumin, coriander,
and paprika with the garlic. Add 1 jalapeño, seeded and chopped, with the
bell pepper. Replace basil with fresh cilantro and add the juice of 1 lemon
to finish. Serve in a bowl over couscous.

variations

black bean stew with eggs

see base recipe page 144

spicy bean soup
Follow the basic recipe, increasing the broth to 3 cups. After removing bay leaves, partly blend the soup with an immersion blender. Omit eggs and serve with a little non-fat sour cream and fresh cilantro.

black bean enchiladas
Follow the basic recipe, omitting the eggs. In a small baking dish, spread 1/2 cup prepared tomato salsa. Put 1/3 cup stew in each of 4 warmed calorie-reduced, whole wheat 7-inch tortillas. Divide between them 2 tablespoons canned green chilies, 1 chopped jalapeño, and 1/4 cup non-fat sour cream. Fold and put in dish seam-side down. Cover with another 1/2 cup salsa, sprinkle with 2 tablespoons low-fat cheese, and bake for 30 minutes.

bean chili
Follow the basic recipe, using 1 (15-ounce) can each of black beans and pinto beans, and 1 (15-ounce) can tomatoes. Brown 1 pound extra-lean ground beef with the garlic and spices. Omit the eggs.

black bean tacos
Make the stew, omitting eggs. Take 4 taco shells, add 3 tablespoons stew, 1 tablespoon each grated low-fat Cheddar cheese, low-fat sour cream and lettuce.

quick-and-easy main dishes

Everyday cooking needn't be a chore. Here's a collection of quick and easy favorites to have on hand, which means you won't be tempted to eat something bad just because you are in a hurry.

easiest-ever slim pizza

see variations page 171

Home-cooked pizza just doesn't get simpler than this. With this amazing quick base, the dough is made and the pizza cooked in well under half an hour. How convenient is that!

pizza
1 cup whole wheat flour
1 cup all-purpose flour
1/4 tsp. salt
1/2 tsp. baking soda
2/3 cup non-fat
   Greek yogurt
2–3 tbsp. water

topping
1 (3 1/2-oz.) jar roasted bell
   peppers, drained
2 canned plum tomatoes
1 tbsp. balsamic vinegar
salt and black pepper
1/8–1/4 tsp. crushed red
   pepper flakes

1 red onion, sliced
2 1/2 oz. prosciutto, torn
2 plum tomatoes, sliced
1 (8-oz.) ball low-fat
   mozzarella cheese, sliced
2 cups arugula, to garnish

Preheat oven to 425°F.

Put both flours, salt, baking soda, and yogurt in a bowl. Either by hand or with the dough hook of an electric mixer, bring the mixture together, using a little water to bind. Knead briefly until the dough is smooth. Roll out to a 12-inch-diameter circle on a piece of lightly floured baking parchment. Don't worry if your circles are not perfectly formed, this adds to the charm. Bake for 10 minutes.

Purée the bell peppers, tomatoes, and vinegar in a food processor. Remove the base from the oven and spread with the sauce; season with salt and pepper. Sprinkle with the crushed red pepper, onion, prosciutto, tomatoes, and mozzarella. Bake for 10 minutes and serve topped with arugula.

Makes 4 servings

crispy fish & fries

see variations page 172

This crispy oven-baked fish and fries recipe is a healthy and delicious reworking of a fatty favorite. Soak your sliced potatoes in water before cooking, then they will be even crisper.

fries
2 large russet potatoes,
    unpeeled, scrubbed
4 tsp. flour
1 egg white
1/2 tsp. garlic powder
1/2 tsp. paprika
salt and black pepper

fish
1 cup fresh bread crumbs
3 tbsp. fresh parsley, chopped
1 tbsp. fresh chives, chopped
1/2 tsp. grated lemon zest
1/2 tbsp. canola oil
4 cod or haddock fillets,
    4–5 oz. each

4 tsp. low-fat mayonnaise
    (page 20)
lemon wedges, to garnish

Preheat oven to 400°F. Lightly spray 2 cookie sheets with low-fat cooking spray.

Slice the potatoes into 1/4- to 1/2-inch-thick wedges. Beat the egg white until just frothy, beat in the garlic powder and paprika, then season with salt and pepper. Toss in the potato wedges, then transfer to a baking sheet, separating the potatoes as much as possible. Bake for 45 minutes, turning every 15 minutes. Meanwhile, combine the bread crumbs, parsley, chives, lemon zest, and oil; season with salt and pepper. Put the fillets skin-side down on a second prepared cookie sheet, spread each with 1 teaspoon mayonnaise, then press the bread crumb mixture into the fish. Put in the oven when the fries have about 15 minutes left to cook. Bake until the flesh is opaque. Serve with the fries, garnished with lemon wedges.

Makes 4 servings

pork steaks with apple & sage

see variations page 173

Pork and apple, a classic combination, is pepped up with a few herbs and some grainy mustard here. For a special occasion, you could substitute 2 tablespoons Calvados for some of the apple juice. This dish is delicious accompanied by steamed cabbage or green beans and a couple of simple boiled potatoes.

4 (5-oz.) pork loin steaks, visible fat removed
salt and black pepper
1/2 tbsp. canola oil or low-fat cooking spray
2 small apples, cored and sliced into 12 pieces
1 onion

1 garlic clove, minced
2 tbsp. chopped fresh sage or 2 tsp. dried
3/4 cup chicken broth
1/2 cup apple juice
1 tbsp. whole-grain mustard

Season the pork with salt and pepper. Heat the oil or spray in a large skillet, then add the pork and cook over medium-high heat for 3–4 minutes, on each side, until golden brown. Remove from the pan and keep warm. Add the apples and onion to the skillet and cook gently for about 5 minutes, stirring occasionally. Add the garlic and sage and cook for 2 more minutes.

Pour in a little broth and deglaze the pan, then add the remaining broth, apple juice, and mustard. Bring to a boil and simmer, uncovered, for 10 minutes, until the sauce is reduced by about one third and the steaks are tender. If the liquid has reduced too much, add a little more broth or water.

Makes 4 servings

grilled lime & chili chicken

see variations page 174

Nothing is nicer than a succulent piece of flavorsome grilled chicken. The instructions here work for an oven broiler or an outside grill, so take your pick depending on the weather! You can put the chicken together with the marinade in a resealable plastic bag for up to 24 hours in the refrigerator, or make up a batch and freeze them in the bags.

1 tsp. lime zest
1/4 cup lime juice
1 tbsp. canola oil
1 tsp. honey or sugar-free maple syrup
1-2 jalapeño chiles, seeded and finely chopped,
    or 2-3 tsp. chili powder

1 garlic clove, minced
1/2 tsp. ground cumin
4 skinless chicken breasts

Combine all the ingredients for the marinade in a bowl or resealable plastic bag. Add the chicken, toss to coat, and marinate for at least 30 minutes, or overnight.

Cook the chicken under the grill or on the barbecue about 4 inches away from the heat source, basting from time to time with the marinade. Turn the chicken after about 8 minutes, then cook for about 7 minutes longer. When the chicken is cooked, it will feel firm and will spring to the touch and the juices will run clear.

Makes 4 servings

oven-baked shrimp & asparagus risotto

see variations page 175

Everyone loves a creamy risotto, and this oven-baked method is very simple to cook.

large pinch saffron strands
3 cups vegetable or chicken broth
1/2 tbsp. canola oil or low-fat cooking spray
3 shallots, finely chopped
4 cloves garlic, finely chopped
1 1/2 cups risotto (Arborio) rice
12 oz. raw medium shrimp, peeled and deveined

1 cup sliced asparagus
4 oz. baby spinach leaves
1 tsp. lemon zest
1 tbsp. lemon juice
2 tbsp. fresh parsley or tarragon, chopped
freshly grated Parmesan, to serve

Preheat oven to 400°F.

Put the saffron in a saucepan with the broth. Bring to a boil, cover, and keep hot. Meanwhile, heat the oil or spray in a Dutch oven, add the shallots, and cook for 2 minutes,. Add the garlic and cook for 1 minute. Add the rice and cook, stirring, until the rice is coated and becoming translucent around the edges. Slowly pour in the hot broth, cover, and bake for 15 minutes until the rice is tender and most of the liquid has been absorbed.

Stir the shrimp, asparagus, spinach, and lemon zest into the risotto. Cover and return to the oven for 15–20 minutes, until all the liquid has been absorbed and the rice is soft. Stir in the lemon juice and parsley or tarragon. Serve immediately with a sprinkling of Parmesan cheese.

Makes 4 servings

szechuan-style pork

see variations page 176

Szechuan-style cooking is known for its spiciness, giving this stir-fry a big burst of flavor. If you like your food with a gentler edge, use fewer chiles. Serve with rice.

10 oz. boneless pork loin, visible fat removed
1/4 cup light, sodium-reduced soy sauce
2 tbsp. cornstarch
2 tbsp. rice wine, dry sherry, or chicken broth
1/2–1 tbsp. canola oil or low-fat cooking spray
1/2–1 tsp. dried red pepper flakes
2 garlic cloves, minced

1 tsp. fresh ginger, shredded
1–4 Thai bird chiles
1 cup carrots, julienned
2 celery stalks, diagonally sliced
1 large red bell pepper, sliced
1 cup savoy cabbage, shredded
3 green onions, diagonally sliced

Cut the pork crosswise into thin slices, then cut each slice into thin strips. Blend 2 tablespoons soy sauce and the cornstarch in a medium bowl, add the pork, and toss to evenly coat. Combine the remaining soy sauce with the rice wine, sherry, or broth, and set aside.

Heat 1/2 tablespoon oil or spray in a wok or large skillet. Add the red pepper flakes and cook until golden brown. Add the pork and stir-fry over medium-high heat for about 5 minutes, until cooked through. Transfer the pork to a warmed bowl and keep warm.

Add the garlic, ginger, and chiles to the pan, and cook for 1 minute. Add the carrots and stir-fry for 1 minute, using a little more oil, or a splash of water, as needed. Repeat this process for the celery, bell pepper, cabbage, and green onion — the vegetables should all be tender-crisp. Return the meat to the pan with the soy mixture and cook for 2 minutes, stirring constantly to heat through.

Makes 4 servings

skinny citrus fish tacos

see variations page 177

This popular dish is enlivened with a bright citrus rub that adds an extra zing to the fish. For best results make the coleslaw at least 4 hours ahead for the flavors to mingle.

coleslaw
1/3 cup non-fat yogurt
3 tbsp. low-fat mayonnaise
(page 20)
1 tbsp. lemon juice
pinch salt
2 cups white or red cabbage,
shredded

fish
4 white fish steaks such as
haddock or mahi-mahi,
about 4–5 oz. each
1/2 tbsp. lemon zest
1/2 tbsp. orange zest
1 tsp. lime zest
1 tsp. paprika

1 tbsp. canola oil
salt and black pepper

to serve
8 tortillas, warmed
2 tomatoes, chopped
fresh cilantro, chopped,
to garnish

To make the coleslaw, combine the yogurt, mayonnaise, lemon juice, and salt in a bowl. Toss in the cabbage and coat evenly with the dressing. Let stand for 4 hours, if possible. Meanwhile, cut each fish steak into 4 pieces. Combine the lemon, orange, and lime zest with the paprika and oil. Season with salt and black pepper. Rub all over the fish and let stand for 30 minutes or up to 4 hours in the refrigerator.

Preheat the broiler and line the broiler pan with aluminum foil and lightly spray with low-fat spray. Put the fish on the foil, skin-side down, and broil for 4–6 minutes on each side until cooked through. Transfer the fish to a warmed plate and cut into large chunks. Fill each tortilla with 4 chunks of fish and top with coleslaw, tomato, and chopped cilantro. Serve while still warm.

Makes 4 servings

linguine with pesto & tomatoes

see variations page 178

The U.S.-recommended pasta portion size of 2 ounces is about 200 calories, so choose your sauce carefully. Pesto is an Italian classic and this version uses minimal quantities of olive oil, Parmesan, and nuts; just don't compromise on quality.

pesto
1 cup fresh basil leaves
1/3 cup Parmesan cheese,
    shredded
2 tbsp. extra-virgin olive oil

1 tbsp. pine nuts
1 tbsp. fresh bread crumbs
1 garlic clove
1/4 tsp. salt

8 oz. spinach linguine
1 tsp. canola oil or non-stick
    spray
1 cup baby plum tomatoes,
    halved

Put all the ingredients for the pesto in a blender or food processor and process until smooth. Alternatively, prepare traditionally by pounding the ingredients until smooth using a pestle and mortar.

Bring a large saucepan of slightly salted water to a boil. When boiling rapidly, add the linguine and cook for about 8 minutes, or according to the package directions, until just cooked (al dente). Drain the pasta, reserving some of the cooking liquid.

At the same time, heat the oil or spray in a small skillet and cook the tomatoes until softened but still holding their shape. To serve, toss the linguine with a little of the reserved cooking liquid to loosen, then toss in the pesto and tomatoes.

Makes 4 servings

quick chicken cacciatore

see variations page 179

Chicken in a rich tomato sauce makes a great family supper and is easy to cook for a crowd. Serve with pasta bows or a small baked potato.

4 skinless boneless chicken breasts
salt and black pepper
1/2 tbsp. canola oil or low-fat cooking spray
1 medium onion, chopped
2 garlic cloves, minced
12 celery stalks, sliced

2 bay leaves
1/2 cup chicken broth
1 (28-oz.) can tomatoes
1 tbsp. tomato paste
2 tsp. dried Italian herbs
4 anchovy fillets or 4 tsp. anchovy paste

Pound the chicken breasts between pieces of plastic wrap until about 1/2-inch thick. Slice into 4 pieces. Season the chicken with salt and pepper. Heat the oil or spray in a large skillet, add half the chicken, and cook over medium-high heat for 3–4 minutes, on each side, until golden brown. Remove from the pan and keep warm. Repeat with the second batch.

Add the onion to the skillet and cook gently for about 5 minutes until softened, stirring occasionally. Add the garlic, celery, and bay leaves, and cook for another minute. Deglaze the pan with the broth. Add the tomatoes, tomato paste, and herbs, and bring to a boil, breaking up the tomatoes. Blot the anchovies on paper towels to remove excess oil, add to the pan, and simmer for 15 minutes, until the sauce is reduced by about one third and the chicken is cooked through. Adjust the seasoning to taste.

Makes 4 servings

tomato & black olive tart

see variations page 180

This impressive-looking tart is very simple to construct and quite delicious. The puréed beans provide a good protein source and give the tart substance.

flour, for dusting
2 garlic cloves
1 (15-oz.) can cannellini
    beans, drained
2 tbsp. skim milk
1/4 cup loose-packed parsley
    leaves
salt and black pepper

olive oil–flavored spray
1 small red onion, cut into
    thin rings
1 tsp. fennel seeds
1 tsp. coriander seeds
1/4 tsp. crushed red pepper
    flakes
4 sheets phyllo pastry

3 large, ripe beefsteak
    tomatoes, sliced
12 black olives, halved
1/4 tsp. sugar
1 tbsp. lemon juice
2 tbsp. fresh basil, chopped

Preheat oven to 400°F. Dust a cookie sheet with flour.

With the food processor motor running, drop in the garlic to chop. Add the beans, milk, and parsley, and process until smooth. Season with salt and pepper. Set aside. Heat olive oil-flavored spray in a small skillet, add the onion, and cook for about 5 minutes, until soft. Add the fennel, coriander, and crushed red pepper, and cook for 2 minutes.

Put a sheet of phyllo on the cookie sheet, lightly coat with spray. Top with a second sheet, spray; repeat with the third; then lay the fourth sheet on top. Spread with the bean purée, leaving a margin around the edges. Sprinkle with the onion mixture and top with tomato slices and olives; season with salt, pepper, and sugar. Bake for 15–20 minutes until the pastry is golden. Sprinkle with the lemon juice. Add the herbs just before serving. Serve hot or cold.

Makes 4–6 servings

curried drumsticks

see variations page 181

This is one of those simple recipes that can be whipped up with next to no effort. The drumsticks are great hot, accompanied by a curried vegetable dish. Wrap them in aluminum foil and they are great for packed lunches too.

2/3 cup non-fat yogurt
2 tbsp. water
2 tbsp. curry paste
1/2 tsp. ground turmeric
1 tsp. lemon zest
8 chicken drumsticks
lemon wedges, optional

dip (optional)
1/3 cup non-fat yogurt
pinch salt
pinch sugar
1/2 tsp. white wine vinegar
1/4 cup fresh mint, chopped

Preheat oven to 400°F.

Mix together the yogurt, water, curry paste, turmeric, and lemon zest. Coat the chicken drumsticks in the mixture and refrigerate for at least 1 hour but no more than 8.

Put in a greased baking dish and bake for 30 minutes. Alternatively, broil or grill for 16–20 minutes, turning occasionally. Serve hot or cold with a lemon wedge or with the dip.

If using the dip, combine all the ingredients in a small bowl until smooth.

Makes 4 servings

easiest-ever slim pizza

see base recipe page 155

broccolini & goat cheese pizza
Follow the basic recipe, omitting prosciutto, mozzarella, and arugula. Instead use 8 ounces blanched broccolini, halved lengthwise; 12 whole black olives; and 6 ounces crumbled goat cheese.

florentine pizza
Follow the basic recipe, omitting prosciutto, mozzarella, and arugula. Put 8 ounces baby spinach in a colander and pour over boiling water to wilt. Drain thoroughly. Put on top of the pizza with a grating of nutmeg. Make 4 slight indentations and carefully crack an egg into each. Sprinkle with 2 tablespoons Parmesan cheese. Bake for 10 minutes or until eggs are just set.

tex-mex chicken pizza
Follow the basic recipe, omitting prosciutto and arugula. Use instead 1 cup shredded cooked chicken, 1 sliced green bell pepper, and 1/2 cup cooked corn. Drizzle with 3/4 cup spicy salsa, cook as directed, and serve garnished with chopped fresh cilantro.

even-faster pizza
Follow the basic recipe, using 4 pita breads or flatbreads instead of pizza base. Bake for 5–6 minutes.

variations

crispy fish & fries

see base recipe page 156

crispy chicken & fries
Follow the basic recipe, using 1 pound chicken tenders instead of fish. Mix the chicken and mayonnaise in a bowl, adding 1 teaspoon skim milk. Toss in the seasoned bread crumbs. Cook as directed, turning the chicken after 8 minutes of cooking time.

crispy shrimp & fries
Follow the basic recipe, using 1 pound raw large shrimp instead of fish. Mix the shrimp and mayonnaise in a bowl, adding 1 teaspoon skim milk. Toss in the seasoned bread crumbs. Put in the oven 10 minutes before the fries are cooked, turn over after 6 minutes, then bake 3–4 minutes, or until cooked through.

crispy creole chicken & sweet potato fries
Prepare the crispy chicken as directed above, adding 1 teaspoon Cajun spices to the bread crumbs. Use scrubbed sweet potatoes instead of potatoes.

pork steaks with apple & sage

see base recipe page 159

turkey with apple & sage
Follow the basic recipe, using turkey breasts instead of pork. Works with chicken breasts too.

pork with pears, ham & sage
Follow the basic recipe, using pears instead of apples and omitting the mustard. Use only half the quantity of broth and apple juice and add the lean meat from 3 torn prosciutto slices with the broth.

pork with balsamic plums
Follow the basic recipe, using 4 plums instead of apples, and omitting the mustard and sage. Use a red rather than yellow onion and 1 sprig rosemary (1/2 teaspoon dried). Reduce the broth by half and add 2 tablespoons balsamic vinegar before serving.

pork with apples, sweet potatoes & sage
Follow the basic recipe, adding 2 medium sweet potatoes, scrubbed and sliced, with the apples. Add 1/2 teaspoon ground cinnamon with the garlic.

variations

grilled lime & chili chicken

see base recipe page 160

lime & chili pork chops
Follow the basic recipe, using 4 boneless 1/2-inch-thick pork chops, with visible fat removed. Cooking time will be about 10 minutes; turn halfway through cooking time.

lime & harissa chicken
Follow the basic recipe, substituting 1–2 teaspoons harissa paste for the jalapeño or chili powder and adding 1/2 teaspoon ground coriander.

lime & yogurt chicken
Follow the basic recipe, but reduce the lime juice to 2 tablespoons and add 1/2 cup non-fat yogurt. Proceed as directed.

lemon & herb chicken
Follow the basic recipe, substituting lemon for the lime and omitting the chiles or chili powder and cumin. Add 1 tablespoon roughly chopped fresh thyme (1 teaspoon dried) and 1 teaspoon chopped fresh rosemary (1/4 teaspoon dried).

oven-baked shrimp & asparagus risotto

see base recipe page 161

oven-baked asparagus risotto with prosciutto
Prepare the basic recipe, omitting the shrimp. Add 4 slices prosciutto, slice
into strips, and drape over the finished mounds of risotto. The heat from the
risotto will warm them through without cooking them. This method works
with smoked salmon too.

oven-baked tomato, pea & asparagus risotto
Follow the basic recipe, omitting shrimp. Add 1 cup frozen peas and 1/2 cup
halved cherry tomatoes with the asparagus. Garnish with chopped fresh
basil, parsley, or chives.

oven-baked seafood risotto
Follow the basic recipe, omitting asparagus and shrimp and using fish broth
instead of chicken broth. Use 1 1/4 pounds prepared mixed raw seafood.

risotto cakes
Prepare the basic recipe. Let the risotto cool, then shape into 12 cakes. Make
a hole in the center of each, press in one small cube of low-fat mozzarella,
and smooth over the hole. Dredge with bread crumbs (about 1 cup). Heat
low-fat spray in a skillet and fry the cakes for 3–4 minutes on each side,
until golden. This is also a good way to use leftover risotto.

variations

szechuan-style pork

see base recipe page 162

szechuan-style tofu

Follow the basic recipe, omitting pork. Mix all the soy sauce with the
cornstarch and rice wine, sherry, or broth; set aside. Take 1 (12-ounce)
package five-spice or oriental-flavored tofu, which has been pressed and
drained. Cut the tofu into 3/4-inch cubes and stir-fry for about 3 minutes
per side until golden. Proceed as directed.

szechuan-style chicken & broccoli

Follow the basic recipe, replacing pork with sliced boneless chicken breast.
Omit the cabbage and add 1 cup broccoli flowerets after the carrots.

szechuan-style fish

Follow the basic recipe, using 12 ounces white fish fillet instead of pork.
Mix all the soy sauce with the cornstarch and rice wine, sherry, or broth.
Set aside. Cut the fish into 1-inch cubes and stir-fry in the hot oil until
opaque. Proceed as for basic recipe.

ginger pork

Follow the basic recipe, omitting chiles and shredded ginger. Substitute
3/4-inch piece fresh ginger, peeled and cut into thin slices.

skinny citrus fish tacos

see base recipe page 165

skinny beef tacos
Make the coleslaw. Omit fish. In a non-stick skillet, dry-fry 12 ounces extra-
lean ground beef. When evenly brown and crumbled, add 1 tablespoon each
garlic powder, chili powder, and ground cumin. Fry for 1 minute, add 1/2 cup
tomato sauce, and cook for 2 minutes. Add 2 chopped green onions. Fill the
tacos as directed.

baha fish tacos
Follow the basic recipe, but instead of the citrus rub make a marinade
with 2 tablespoons lime juice; 1/2 tablespoon canola oil; 2 teaspoons
chili powder; 3/4 teaspoon each ground cumin, ground coriander, and
garlic powder; and a pinch of salt. Proceed as directed, draining the fish
before cooking.

skinny chicken tacos
Follow the basic recipe, using 12 ounces chicken tenders. Broil for 5–8
minutes on each side until cooked through. Shred, then fill tacos as directed.

seared scallop tacos
Follow the basic recipe, using 12 prepared scallops instead of fish. Heat low-
fat cooking spray in a skillet and cook scallops for 2–5 minutes, until
opaque; cut each into four. Sprinkle with lemon juice, then use to fill tacos.

variations

linguine with pesto & tomatoes

see base recipe page 166

cilantro & pumpkin seed pesto with linguine & tomatoes
Follow the basic recipe, substituting cilantro for the basil and toasted
pumpkin seeds for the pine nuts. Add 1 tablespoon lemon juice and
1/4 teaspoon cracked coriander seeds to the pesto before blending.

arugula & walnut pesto with linguine
Follow the basic recipe, substituting arugula for the basil and 2 tablespoons
toasted walnuts for the pine nuts.

kale & walnut pesto with linguine
Follow the basic recipe, substituting kale for the basil and 2 tablespoons
toasted walnuts for the pine nuts. Add 1 tablespoon lemon juice and
1 teaspoon balsamic vinegar to the pesto.

linguine with pesto, ricotta & roasted peppers
Follow the basic recipe, adding 1/2 cup low-fat ricotta cheese to cooked
pasta and using half the quantity of pesto. Omit the tomatoes and use
1 (7-ounce) jar of roasted red peppers, drained and sliced.

variations

quick chicken cacciatore

see base recipe page 167

slow chicken cacciatore
Use 4 small chicken legs instead of breasts. Do not pound, but brown as instructed in a Dutch oven. Do not simmer; instead, cover and cook in a 325°F oven for 45 minutes.

pork cacciatore
Follow the basic recipe, using 12 ounces pork tenderloin instead of chicken breasts. Cut the tenderloin into 1/2-inch pieces, then pound until 1/4 inch thick. Flash-fry for 1–2 minutes on each side to cook through.

chicken & basil cacciatore
Follow the basic recipe, but omit mixed Italian herbs. Add 1 teaspoon lemon zest to the tomato sauce. Just before serving, add 1/4 cup roughly chopped fresh basil.

chicken & mozzarella cacciatore
Follow the basic recipe, using only 3 chicken breasts. When the dish is cooked, add 8 ounces roughly chopped low-fat mozzarella cheese to the sauce. Cook for 1 minute to heat through without melting, then serve immediately.

variations

tomato & black olive tart

see base recipe page 169

tomato & anchovy tart

Prepare the basic recipe, replacing olives with anchovies. Drain a 2-ounce can of anchovies thoroughly, pat dry with paper towel, and arrange decoratively over the tomatoes. Bake as directed.

tomato & spinach tart

Prepare the basic recipe, adding 1/2 pound baby spinach leaves. Put spinach in a colander and pour over boiling water to wilt. Cool slightly and squeeze to drain off excess liquid. Arrange the spinach over the bean paste on the tart and top with tomatoes. Olives are optional.

tomato, black olive & ricotta tart

Prepare the basic recipe. Drop 2/3 cup low-fat ricotta in teaspoonfuls decoratively over the tomatoes, then decorate with the olives. Bake as directed.

tomato & black olive tartlets

Prepare the basic recipe, but use 4 plum tomatoes. Cut the prepared phyllo stack into quarters and put on the cookie sheet. Construct the tartlets as directed, dividing the ingredients between the tartlets, leaving a 1/4-inch margin around the edges. Bake for 15 minutes, or until golden.

curried drumsticks

see base recipe page 170

crisp curried drumsticks
Marinate drumsticks, then roll in 1 cup soft bread crumbs. Put in the baking dish and give them one spray of low-fat cooking oil. Bake as directed.

turkish curried drumsticks
Follow the basic recipe, using these marinade ingredients: 1 minced garlic clove, 2/3 cup yogurt, 1 tablespoon lemon juice, 1 teaspoon shredded fresh ginger, 1 teaspoon each hot paprika and dried mint, and 1/4 teaspoon salt.

chicken curry
Marinate the chicken as directed. Spray a Dutch oven with low-fat cooking oil and gently cook 1 chopped onion for 5 minutes. Add 2 cloves garlic, 3 whole green chiles, and 1 teaspoon garam masala, and cook for 1 minute. Add the chicken; 2 large skinned, seeded, and chopped tomatoes; and 1 1/4 cups chicken broth. Bring to a boil and simmer for 40 minutes. Stir in another 1/2 teaspoon garam masala before serving.

curried lamb kebabs
Omit chicken. Marinate 12 ounces lean cubed lamb. Thread onto skewers, alternating with cherry tomatoes (12 in total) and wedges made from 1 green bell pepper. Broil or grill for 8–10 minutes on each side.

main dishes to impress

It is good to have on hand some recipes that will
wow your guests without ruining your diet or
theirs. The following selection caters to all tastes
and different occasions — the roast ham is great as
a centerpiece for a big event, the five-spice chicken
is a delicious and simple after-work supper, and the
roulade makes a sophisticated vegetarian offering.

five-spice chicken with bok choy

see variations page 200

This dish is extremely flexible as you can prepare to the end of step two several hours in advance. Just cool and keep refrigerated until required.

1 tsp. five-spice powder
1 tsp. fish sauce
1 tbsp. light soy sauce
1 tbsp. brown sugar
1/8 tsp. pepper
1 tsp. crushed red pepper flakes
1/2 cup water

4 large boneless, skinless
   chicken thighs
1/2 – 1 tbsp. canola oil, or
   low-fat cooking spray
3 shallots, sliced
2 garlic cloves, minced

2 bok choy, stalks sliced
   horizontally, leaves
   shredded
1 small red bell pepper
salt
green onion, to garnish
red chile, to garnish

In a bowl, combine the first seven ingredients; set aside. Slice the chicken crosswise into strips. Heat 1 teaspoon oil or spray in a large skillet, then cook the chicken in batches, without crowding, over medium-high heat, until browned. Set aside and keep warm.

Add 1 teaspoon oil or spray the pan and stir-fry the shallot for 2 minutes. Add the garlic, cook for 1 minute. Add the seasoning mixture and bring to a boil. Add the chicken and simmer for 15 minutes, until cooked through. (If preparing in advance, cool, and refrigerate overnight at this point.)

Just before serving, bring the pan of chicken to a boil, then reduce heat to simmer. (If you are reheating this dish, you will probably have to add 2–4 tablespoons water.) Add the bok choy stalks and simmer for about 3 minutes to soften. Add the bok choy leaves and bell pepper and cook for 2 more minutes. Salt to taste and serve with rice garnished with green onion and chile.

Makes 4 servings

chipotle-tangerine glazed steaks

see variations page 201

Not only does this marinade give this steak a wonderful zing, it tenderizes it too. The variations provide several other marinades for you to try. Serve with a salad or a steamed green vegetable such as broccoli.

4 lean steaks, sirloin or rib eye
(about 4–5 oz. each)

glaze
1/2 cup tangerine juice
2 tbsp. chipotle in adobo sauce,
chopped

2 tbsp. low-sodium soy sauce
2 tbsp. sugar-free maple syrup
1 garlic clove, minced

Trim the steaks of all visible fat.

Combine all the ingredients for the glaze. Brush the glaze all over the steaks, cover, and set aside to marinate for at least 1 hour.

Preheat grill or broiler to high. Shake off and reserve excess marinade from steaks. Cook about 3 inches from the heat source for 1 1/2–4 minutes on each side, or until done to your liking. Use any excess marinade to baste the cooking steaks. Let rest in a warm place for 5 minutes before serving. This is essential as it allows the meat to relax and become more tender.

Makes 4 servings

goat cheese & cranberry pork

see variations page 202

In this elegant dish, the lean pork tenderloin benefits from the cheese-based stuffing, which adds moisture as it cooks and the cranberry sauce, which adds a piquant note.

1 (1-lb.) pork tenderloin
salt and black pepper

4 oz. goat cheese, sliced
1/4 cup bread crumbs
3 tbsp. fresh sage leaves,
　chopped
2 tbsp. fresh parsley, chopped
1 garlic clove, minced

salt and black pepper
1/2 tbsp. oil or low-fat
　cooking spray
8–10 whole fresh sage leaves
sprig fresh rosemary

sauce
1/4 cup water
1/4 cup balsamic vinegar

1 tbsp. grainy mustard
1/3 cup frozen cranberries
1 tbsp. fresh sage, chopped
1/2 tbsp. fresh rosemary,
　chopped
1–2 tsp. sugar-free maple
　syrup
salt and black pepper

Preheat oven to 350°F.

Trim the tenderloin of visible fat, score in half lengthwise, but not all the way through, and flatten out. Pound between pieces of plastic wrap until it is 1/4 to 1/2 inch thick. Season with salt and pepper.

Lay slices of goat cheese along the middle of the tenderloin, leaving a gap at each end. Combine the bread crumbs, sage, parsley, garlic, salt, and pepper, and sprinkle over the cheese. Close up the meat, enclosing the filling at both ends. Tie with string to secure. Heat the oil or spray in a heavy, ovenproof, covered skillet. When really hot, sear the pork briefly on all sides to brown. Lay the sage leaves over the meat and put the rosemary on top. Transfer the skillet to the oven, cover, and cook for about 45 minutes or until the pork is cooked through (155°F internal temperature).

Remove the meat from the oven, put on a warmed platter, cover with foil, and set aside to rest in a warm place. Meanwhile, over medium heat, add the water to the skillet and scrape the bottom to deglaze. Reduce by half, then stir in the vinegar and mustard, bring to a boil, and add the cranberries and rosemary. Season to taste with maple syrup, salt, and pepper. Return to a boil and cook for a few minutes until the cranberries have burst and the sauce is thick.

Cut the twine from the pork or remove toothpicks, discard the rosemary, lay the sage back over the pork, and serve with the sauce.

Makes 4 servings

steak & shitake teriyaki

see variations page 203

Using soba noodles reduces the calories by about one-third over regular egg noodles.

marinade
1/2 cup low-sodium soy sauce
2 tbsp. mirin
2 tbsp. water
2 tbsp. honey
1 tsp. sesame oil
2 tsp. fresh ginger, minced
1 garlic clove, sliced

12 oz. steak, rump or flank
1/2 tsp. sesame oil
3–5 tsp. canola oil
1 8-oz. package soba noodles
1 small onion, sliced
6 oz. broccoli florets

8 oz. shitake mushrooms,
    sliced, tough stems
    removed
4 oz. enoki mushrooms,
    trimmed
1 tbsp. sesame seeds

Combine the marinade ingredients in a bowl. Thinly slice the steak across the grain and cut into strips. Toss with the marinade. Cover and refrigerate for at least 2 hours or overnight. Drain the beef, reserving the marinade, and pat dry on paper towels. Heat the sesame oil and half the canola oil in a wok or skillet. Add half the beef and cook over medium-high heat until browned. Remove from the pan, keep warm, and repeat with the remaining beef.

Meanwhile, boil a saucepan of water for the soba noodles and cook for 5 minutes, or according to the package directions. Drain and keep warm. Add the remaining oil to the wok or skillet and stir-fry the onion and broccoli for 3 minutes, add the shitake mushrooms and stir-fry for 2 minutes, then add the enoki mushrooms and stir-fry for 1 more minute. Add the steak with the reserved marinade and reheat. Serve with the soba noodles and garnish with the sesame seeds.

Makes 4 servings

sole en papillote

see variations page 204

Perfect for entertaining, your fish and vegetables are all packaged in individual parcels, refrigerated and popped into the oven half an hour before required.

2 medium carrots, cut into 2-inch julienne
2 small leeks, white part only, cut into
    2-inch julienne
1 medium zucchini, cut into 2-inch julienne
1 garlic clove, minced
4 tbsp. white wine or fish broth
1 tsp. fennel seeds

salt and black pepper
4 (4- to 6-oz.) sole fillets or other flatfish fillets
1/2 tsp. paprika
2 tbsp. fresh chives, chopped
4 medium shrimp in shells
1 lemon, cut into 8 wedges
8 small sprigs thyme

Preheat oven to 400°F.

Cut 4 pieces of baking parchment large enough to accommodate the fish fillets generously. Divide the vegetables between the parcels, sprinkle over the wine and fennel seeds, then season with salt and pepper. Put the fish on top, season with salt and paprika, and sprinkle with chives. Lay the shrimp, lemon wedges, and thyme sprigs on top.

Bring together the edges of the parchment, roll over and fold securely to seal the parcel, twisting the ends together. Refrigerate, if not cooking immediately.

Put the parcels on a cookie sheet and bake for 12–15 minutes, depending on thickness of the fish. Remove from oven and rest for 2 minutes. Put on warmed plates, carefully break the seal on the packages, then serve immediately in the paper.

Makes 4 servings

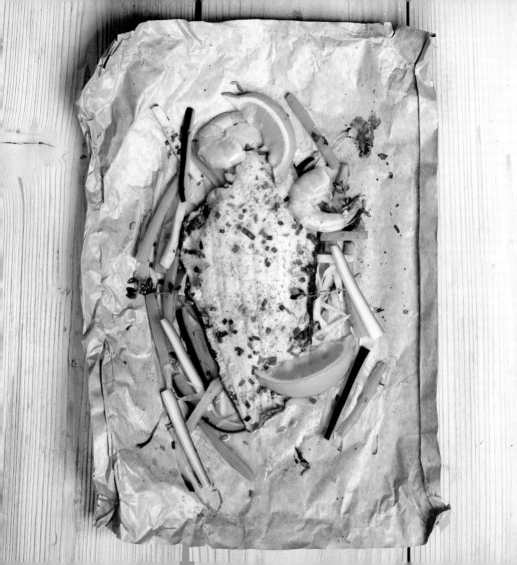

maple–mustard glazed ham

see variations page 205

This is the dish to cook for a crowd — the perfect centerpiece. It is wrong to think that ham is a fatty meat; you just need to cut off the visible fat before eating. It is excellent served hot with vegetables and equally good served cold as a salad.

1 (8- to 10-lb.) bone-in fresh smoked or
   unsmoked ham
2 tbsp. whole cloves (optional)

3/4 cup sugar-free maple syrup
1/4 cup grainy mustard
2 tbsp. Worcestershire sauce

The day before cooking, put the ham in a stockpot of cold water and soak overnight, changing the water once. Drain and dry.

Preheat oven to 350°F. Put the ham in a large roasting pan and cover tightly with aluminum foil. Bake for 3 hours.

Remove ham from the oven and, with a sharp knife, cut off the rind, leaving about 1/4 inch fat around the ham. Score a diamond pattern into this fat layer, taking care not to cut into the flesh. If you want, press a clove into the center of each diamond. Mix together the maple syrup, mustard, and Worcestershire sauce and rub into the ham. Return to the oven and roast, uncovered, for 30 minutes, basting occasionally until the ham is tender and the coating caramelized. When done, a meat thermometer should register 140°F.

Makes about 12 servings

persian spiced turkey loaf

see variations page 206

This wonderfully fragrant Middle Eastern–inspired loaf owes its origins to the spicy ground lamb dishes of the region, but is given a lighter twist by using ground turkey.

1/2 tbsp. canola oil or low-fat cooking spray
1 large onion, finely chopped
4 garlic cloves, minced
4 tsp. ground sumac
2 tsp. ground cumin
1 1/4 lb. lean ground turkey
1 egg, beaten

4 tsp. harissa paste
1/3 cup pine nuts, toasted
1/3 cup pumpkin seeds, toasted
1/4 cup fresh bread crumbs
2 small preserved lemons
salt and black pepper
1 tomato, sliced

Preheat oven to 350°F. Grease and base-line an 8x4-inch loaf pan with parchment paper.

Heat the oil or spray in a small skillet and add the onion, cook for 5 minutes, stirring occasionally, until translucent and turning golden. Add the garlic, cook for 1 minute, then stir in the sumac and cumin and cook, stirring, for another minute. Remove from the heat.

Put the turkey in a bowl and add the egg, harissa paste, pine nuts, pumpkin seeds, bread crumbs, and the chopped rind of the preserved lemons (discard the flesh). Stir in the spicy onion mixture and season generously with salt and pepper. Press into the prepared pan and top with tomato slices. Bake for 50–55 minutes, until cooked through (internal temperature 165°). Remove from the oven and stand for 5 minutes before serving.

Makes 4–5 servings

eggplant parmigiana

see variations page 207

This skinny version uses oven-baked eggplants to keep down the fat content.

2 egg whites
2 tsp. water
2 1/2 lb. eggplant, cut into 1/4-inch-thick slices
1/2 cup dry bread crumbs or crushed crackers
olive oil cooking spray
1 (15-oz.) can tomato sauce
1 tbsp. balsamic vinegar
2 tbsp. chopped sun-dried tomatoes

2 green onions, chopped
1 tsp. garlic paste
pinch sugar
3 tbsp. fresh basil, chopped (or 3 tsp. dried)
1 tbsp. fresh parsley, chopped
salt and black pepper
4 oz. low-calorie mozzarella cheese
1/3 cup freshly grated Parmesan cheese

Preheat oven to 400°F. Line 2 cookie sheets with foil and spray with cooking spray.

In a wide flat bowl, beat the egg whites and water until light and foamy. Put the bread crumbs on a plate. Dip the eggplant in the egg whites, then in bread crumbs. Transfer to the cookie sheet. Lightly spray the eggplant slices with olive oil cooking spray and bake for 20 minutes, until golden. Remove and reduce the heat to 350°F.

Meanwhile, combine the tomato sauce, vinegar, sun-dried tomatoes, green onions, garlic paste, sugar, basil, and parsley in a bowl; season with salt and pepper. Put one third of this mixture in the base of an oiled baking dish, top with a layer of eggplant, half of the crumbled mozzarella and 1 tablespoon Parmesan cheese. Repeat, ending with the tomato sauce. Sprinkle with remaining Parmesan. Bake for 25 minutes or until the cheese is golden.

Makes 4 servings

spinach & antipasto roulade

see variations page 208

Such a healthy combination of ingredients and so low in calories. Mix and match the filling according to what you enjoy most. All you need is an interesting salad on the side.

1 tbsp. canola oil (do not use spray)
12 oz. fresh spinach
2 green onions, roughly chopped
3 tbsp. flour
3 eggs, separated

2 egg whites
2 tbsp. low-fat sour cream
1/4 tsp. ground nutmeg
salt and black pepper

filling
1 cup jarred roasted red

peppers, in brine, sliced
1/4 cup sun-dried tomatoes, rehydrated and chopped
4 jarred marinated artichokes, drained and sliced
2 tbsp. fresh basil leaves, roughly chopped

Preheat oven to 375°F. Line a jellyroll pan with parchment paper.

Cook the spinach in a saucepan of boiling water for 2 minutes until wilted; drain well and cool. Put in a food processor with the green onion, flour, egg yolks, sour cream, and nutmeg. Season with salt and pepper. Process until smooth.

In a separate clean, dry bowl, beat the 5 egg whites until stiff. Using a large metal spoon, stir one third of the beaten egg whites into the spinach. Repeat twice, folding in gently until combined. Pour into the prepared pan and bake for 20–25 minutes until set. Cool in the pan for a few minutes before inverting onto a clean kitchen towel and removing the lining. Roll the roulade up in the towel; cool. To construct, unroll the roulade and lay the red peppers, tomatoes, artichokes, and basil evenly over the top. Carefully roll up the roulade, lifting the towel as you roll. Transfer to a serving plate with the seam facing down.

Makes 4 servings

herb-crusted trout

see variations page 209

This delicious fish dish couldn't be quicker or easier. It takes just 5 minutes to prepare and just 10 minutes or so to cook. Prepare the fish before your guests arrive and keep chilled until required.

1/4 cup fresh parsley leaves
1/4 cup fresh cilantro leaves
2 slices whole wheat bread
zest of 1 lemon
1 tbsp. canola oil
2 tbsp. ground almonds

4 trout fillets
salt and black pepper
4 bunches baby tomatoes on the vine
    or 1 cup baby tomatoes
balsamic vinegar

Preheat broiler to high. Line broiler pan with foil and spray with low-fat cooking spray.

Put the trout fillets skin-side down on the broiler pan and season with salt and pepper, to taste.

Put the parsley and cilantro in a food processor and roughly chop. Roughly tear the bread and add with the lemon zest, oil, and almonds. Process until the bread is in crumbs. Press the mixture onto the top of the trout fillets.

Brush the tomatoes lightly with balsamic vinegar and add to the broiler pan. Cook under the hot broiler for 5–8 minutes, depending on the thickness of the trout. When done, the flesh should be opaque throughout. Turn the tomatoes occasionally while cooking.

Makes 4 servings

variations

five-spice chicken with bok choy

see base recipe page 183

five-spice chicken with mixed vegetables
Follow the basic recipe, replacing the bok choy with I (8-ounce) package of mixed stir-fry vegetables.

five-spice pork with bok choy
Follow the basic recipe, replacing the chicken with 1 pound lean pork cut into 1/2-inch strips.

baked five-spice chicken
Make the seasoning as directed. Leave the chicken pieces whole. Marinate the chicken in the seasoning for at least 1 hour or overnight. Put chicken and seasoning in a baking dish, cover, and cook in a preheated 350°F oven for about 40 minutes, until the chicken is cooked through, basting occasionally. Omit bok choy and bell pepper.

star anise honey chicken with bok choy
Omit the seasoning. Brown the chicken. With the garlic, add 1 tablespoon minced fresh ginger. Then add 1/4 cup each water and light soy sauce, 2 tablespoons orange juice, 1 teaspoon honey, and 1 star anise. Bring to a boil, add browned chicken, and proceed as with base recipe.

variations

chipotle–tangerine glazed steaks

see base recipe page 185

chipotle–tomato glazed steaks
Follow the basic recipe, substituting 1 tablespoon tomato paste,
1 tablespoon lemon juice, and 2 tablespoons water for the tangerine
juice. Marinate and cook the steaks as directed.

balsamic steaks
Follow the basic recipe, replacing the tangerine glaze with a balsamic
marinade. Combine 1/4 cup each soy sauce and balsamic vinegar,
2 tablespoons Worcestershire sauce, 2 teaspoons each of Dijon mustard
and minced garlic, and black pepper to taste.

lemon–garlic–pepper steaks
Follow the basic recipe, replacing the tangerine glaze with a marinade made
by mixing 3 tablespoons lemon juice; 2 tablespoons water; and 1 teaspoon
each canola oil, cracked black pepper, minced garlic, and lemon zest. Season
with salt to taste.

cajun steaks
Follow the basic recipe, replacing the tangerine glaze with a Cajun marinade.
Combine 3 tablespoons each lime juice and water; 2 teaspoons each minced
garlic and canola oil; and 1 1/2 teaspoons Cajun seasoning. Season with salt
to taste.

variations

goat cheese & cranberry pork

see base recipe page 186

goat cheese stuffed turkey breast
Follow the basic recipe, replacing the pork with a 1 1/2-pound turkey breast and making one and a half times the quantity of stuffing.

goat cheese & pumpkin stuffed cranberry pork
Follow the basic recipe, replacing the bread crumbs with 1 cup cooked mashed pumpkin. Spread over the pork, top with the goat cheese, and roll up the meat.

gremolata stuffed cranberry pork
Follow the basic recipe, omitting goat cheese and sage. For the stuffing, increase the bread crumbs to 1/2 cup and stir in the garlic, 3 tablespoons chopped parsley, and 1 teaspoon each olive oil, lemon zest, and lemon juice. Season with salt and black pepper.

mushroom & goat cheese cranberry pork
Follow the basic recipe, adding 2 halved and sliced portobello mushrooms, cooked in hot sauté pan with olive oil spray, to the stuffing layers.

steak & shitake teriyaki

see base recipe page 189

chicken, bamboo & mushroom teriyaki

Follow the basic recipe, using chicken breast instead of steak, ensuring
the chicken is cooked through, 4–5 minutes stir-frying time. Omit enoki
mushrooms and add 1 (8-ounce) can sliced bamboo shoots.

shrimp & shitake teriyaki

Follow the basic recipe, using 12 ounces peeled and deveined raw medium
shrimp instead of steak. Be certain the shrimp are opaque and cooked
through, 4–5 minutes stir-frying time. Proceed as directed.

teriyaki tofu with mushrooms

Follow the basic recipe, omitting steak and using 1 (12-ounce) package tofu,
which has been pressed and drained. Cut the tofu into cubes and marinate
as for steak. Drain and stir-fry until golden all over. Proceed as directed.

barbecued teriyaki steak skewers

Follow the basic recipe, omitting the vegetables, noodles, and sesame seeds.
Thinly slice the steak across the grain and marinate as directed. Soak
8 bamboo skewers in water. Preheat grill to medium-high. Weave each piece
of steak onto the skewers, piercing three times to secure. Grill the skewers for
2 minutes on each side, brushing with the marinade as they cook.

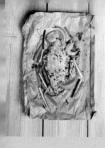

variations

sole en papillote

see base recipe page 190

sole in fennel parcels
Follow the basic recipe, replacing the leeks and zucchini with shredded
fennel and 4 medium tomatoes, skinned, seeded, and finely sliced. Use
crushed coriander seeds instead of fennel seeds and dill instead of chives.

fish & shellfish parcels
Follow the basic recipe, using 4 (2-ounce) chunks of white fish fillet, such as
cod, and 4 ounces each of medium shrimp and shelled clams.

asian fish in parcels
Follow the basic recipe, adding 1 teaspoon minced fresh ginger and 1–2
seeded and shredded jalapeño chiles. Replace wine with 4 tablespoons light
soy sauce and 1/2 teaspoon sesame oil. Use lime instead of lemon and kaffir
lime leaves instead of thyme.

chicken en papillote
Follow the basic recipe, using 1 (6-ounce) skinned and boned chicken breast
per parcel instead of the sole and shrimp. Omit the fennel seeds. Use chicken
broth, not fish broth.

maple–mustard glazed ham

see base recipe page 192

quick & easy maple–mustard glazed ham
To cut down preparation, use a 4- to 5-pound precooked ham. Trim the fat
as needed. Score the ham as directed, stud with cloves, and bake, uncovered,
for about 45 minutes. Brush the meat with the glaze and cook for 30 minutes
more or until a meat thermometer registers 140°F.

orange marmalade glazed ham
Follow the basic recipe, replacing the glaze with a combination of 3/4 cup
sugar-free orange marmalade and 1 teaspoon five-spice powder.

baked ham with pineapple
Follow the basic recipe. When the maple–mustard glaze has been rubbed
into the meat, top with slices of pineapple from a 15-ounce can before
returning to the oven.

cider-baked ham
Soak the ham as directed, then put in roasting pan. In a small saucepan,
combine 2 cups apple cider, 1 cinnamon stick, 1 teaspoon whole cloves,
1/2 teaspoon allspice, and 2 bay leaves. Bring to a boil, then pour over the
ham, cover, and bake, basting every 30 minutes with the cider mixture.
Omit the glaze.

variations

persian spiced turkey loaf

see base recipe page 193

persian spiced meatballs
Follow the basic recipe, omitting tomatoes, but roll mixture into meatballs
and put on a parchment-lined cookie sheet. Bake for 30 minutes until
browned and cooked through. Serve stuffed in pita bread or with a salad.

persian spiced meat loaf
Follow the basic recipe, using 8 ounces ground turkey and 6 ounces each
lean ground lamb and lean ground steak.

simple turkey loaf
Omit the spices, seeds, and preserved lemon. Increase the bread crumbs
to 1/2 cup and season with 1/4 cup ketchup and 2 teaspoons each
Worcestershire sauce and Dijon mustard. Bake as directed.

nutty sage & apple turkey loaf
Omit the sumac, cumin, harissa, preserved lemon, and tomatoes. Increase the
bread crumbs to 1/2 cup and season with 3 tablespoons chopped sage leaves
(3 teaspoons dried); 1 tablespoon Worcestershire sauce; and 1 large Granny
Smith apple, peeled, cored, and shredded.

variations

eggplant parmigiana

see base recipe page 195

zucchini parmigiana
Follow the basic recipe, using zucchini instead of eggplant. Cut the zucchini in 3–5 lengthwise slices depending on thickness.

chicken parmigiana
Follow the basic recipe, replacing eggplant with 4 boneless and skinless chicken breasts or 1-pound chicken tenders, pounded to 1/3-inch thickness. Cut into 3-inch pieces. Proceed as directed.

ground turkey parmigiana
Follow the basic recipe, using 12 ounces ground turkey instead of eggplant. Heat a skillet and brown turkey all over, stirring. Add 1/2 teaspoon ground cinnamon and season with salt and pepper. Layer the tomatoes and cheese alternately with the turkey and cook as directed.

fish parmigiana
Omit the eggplant and mozzarella, and prepare a half portion of the tomato sauce. Dip 4 (5- to 6-ounce) tilapia or other white fish fillets in egg white and bread crumbs. Put in a baking dish big enough to hold the fish in one layer and bake for about 10 minutes, turning once. Top each fillet with tomato sauce and sprinkle with Parmesan cheese. Bake for another 15 minutes.

variations

spinach & antipasto roulade

see base recipe page 196

warm spinach & antipasto roulade
Follow the basic recipe, but do not allow roulade to cool. Warm the antipasto for 1 minute in the microwave and arrange on top of the warm roulade. Carefully roll up and serve at once.

spinach & cottage cheese roulade
Follow the basic recipe, replacing filling with 8 ounces cottage cheese, 2 tablespoons chopped chives, and 1/2 cup halved baby tomatoes.

spinach & smoked trout roulade
Follow the basic recipe, replacing filling with 6 ounces low-fat ricotta cheese; 2 chopped smoked trout fillets mixed with 1 tablespoon each of lemon juice and capers; and 3 chopped green onions.

mushroom & antipasto roulade
Omit the spinach. Spray a sauté pan with low-fat spray and cook 4 ounces finely chopped portobello or cremini mushrooms until tender; cool. Follow the basic instructions using the mushrooms instead of the spinach.

herb-crusted trout

see base recipe page 199

cod with herby crust
Make the topping as directed. Put 4 cod fillets, skin-side up, on the pan and broil for 3 minutes. Turn, press the stuffing into the top of the fish, and broil for about 5 minutes until cooked through and opaque. This works with any chunky white fish fillet.

trout with pesto sesame crust
Prepare the fish as directed. For the topping, combine 4 tablespoons pesto and 3 tablespoons each of sesame seeds and bread crumbs.

trout with herby prosciutto crust
Prepare the basic recipe, adding 2 slices chopped prosciutto, visible fat removed, to the topping mixture.

trout with pistachio crust
Prepare the basic recipe. For the topping, substitute 1/4 cup pistachios for the almonds, use lime instead of lemon, and use only 1 1/2 slices of bread.

on the side

When calories are precious, side dishes have to earn
their keep both as a complement to the main dish
and nutritionally too. The following vegetable dishes
have big bold flavors and work well with a simple
meat or fish dish. Many could also be used as a
light meal or vegetarian main course.

spaghetti squash with parmesan

see variations page 226

Pasta is high in calories, so substitute vegetables for pasta wherever possible. Spaghetti squash is the most obvious substitute, and several unusual suggestions are in the variations. The squash can be served cooked as directed below, then served with tomato-based pasta sauces or used as a base for many light pasta dishes. It doesn't work so well with heavy béchamel sauces.

1 (3-4 lb.) spaghetti squash
3 tbsp. low-fat olive oil spread or butter
2 garlic cloves, minced

salt and black pepper
2 tbsp. fresh sage or parsley, chopped
2 tbsp. Parmesan cheese

Preheat oven to 350°F.

Cut the squash in half lengthwise and scoop out the seeds. Put in a baking dish, cut-side down. Pierce the skin all over with a fork. Bake for 1 hour; cool for 10 minutes.

Turn the cooked squash over and use a fork to draw out the spaghetti-like strands.

In a large saucepan, melt the olive oil spread or butter, and cook the garlic, stirring often, for 2 minutes. Toss in the squash strands and season with salt, pepper, and sage or parsley. Serve sprinkled with Parmesan cheese.

Makes 4 servings

fennel & pepper bake

see variations page 227

This full-flavored side dish works particularly well with simply cooked fish, chicken, or pork. It can also be adapted as a vegetarian main course (see variations).

2 medium or 3 small fennel bulbs, sliced
1/2 tbsp. canola oil or low-fat cooking spray
1 large onion, chopped
4 garlic cloves, minced
1 tsp. coriander seeds

1/2 tsp. fennel seeds
2 red bell peppers, sliced
1 (15-oz.) can crushed tomatoes
1 tbsp. lemon juice
salt and black pepper

Preheat oven to 350°F.

In a saucepan of boiling water, blanch the fennel for 3 minutes, drain, and set aside.

Heat the oil or spray in an ovenproof skillet, add the onion, and cook for 5 minutes, stirring occasionally, until translucent and turning golden. Add the garlic and cook for 1 minute. Lightly crush the coriander and fennel seeds in a pestle and mortar. Add to the skillet and cook for 1 minute. Add the red bell peppers and cook for 2 minutes. Pour in the tomatoes and lemon juice and season with salt and plenty of black pepper.

Add the fennel to the skillet, cover, and bake in the oven for 30 minutes, until the fennel is tender and the tomato sauce thickened.

Makes 4 servings

parmesan roasted brussels sprouts

see variations page 228

This rich and nutritious vegetable is fantastic roasted, which brings out its earthy richness. Choose evenly sized Brussels sprouts so that they cook at the same rate; the smaller the sprout, the better the flavor.

1 lb. small-medium Brussels sprouts, trimmed
   and outer leaves removed
1 tbsp. olive oil
salt and black pepper

3 tbsp. fresh bread crumbs
1 tsp. orange zest
2 tbsp. Parmesan cheese, shredded

Preheat oven to 400°F. Spray a jelly roll pan with low-fat cooking spray.

In a bowl, toss together the Brussels sprouts, olive oil, and salt and pepper. When evenly coasted, toss in the bread crumbs and orange zest. Put Brussels sprouts in a single layer on the prepared pan. Bake for 20 minutes, stirring halfway through cooking. The edges of the sprouts should become lightly browned and the bread crumbs golden. Sprinkle with the Parmesan cheese to serve.

Makes 4 servings

skinnier garlicky mashed potatoes

see variations page 229

This version of mashed potatoes cuts down on the fat without sacrificing the flavor, by exploiting the richness of Yukon gold potatoes and pairing with roast garlic. Potatoes themselves are calorie-rich, so be aware of portion size and look at the variations for other options.

6 garlic cloves, skin on
1 1/2 pounds Yukon gold potatoes, peeled and quartered
1/2 cup low-fat buttermilk, warmed

2 tbsp. low-fat sour cream, room temperature
1 tablespoon fresh chives, snipped
salt and black pepper

Preheat oven to 400°F.

Wrap the garlic cloves in aluminum foil and roast for about 30 minutes until soft when pressed. (You can do this in advance when the oven is on for other dishes.)

Put the potatoes in a saucepan of cold water, bring to a boil, cover, and simmer for about 20 minutes until cooked through. Do not undercook. Drain and return to the saucepan. Squeeze the roasted garlic out of the skins and add to the potatoes. Using a hand masher, mash until no lumps remain. Do not use a food processor or your potatoes will be gluey. Add three quarters of the buttermilk and the sour cream, and beat until smooth, adding the remaining buttermilk, if required, to attain a creamy consistency. Add the chives and season generously to taste.

Makes 6 servings

steamed cabbage with prosciutto & lemon

see variations page 230

Cabbage has bad press and is commonly associated with bad institutional meals. When lightly cooked, however, it is utterly wonderful with complementary flavors such as salty ham, tart lemon, and sublime dill. This simple dish is finished in minutes and will convert the most reluctant.

4 thin slices prosciutto or other air-dried ham	2 tbsp. lemon juice
1/2 head green cabbage, shredded	salt and black pepper
1 tbsp. fresh dill, chopped (or 1 tsp. dried dill)	

In a large skillet, spread out the prosciutto and dry-fry until crispy, about 3 minutes. Tear into pieces.

Meanwhile, put the cabbage in a steamer over boiling water. Sprinkle with dried dill.

Cover and steam for 5–7 minutes until just tender; do not overcook. Put in a warmed serving dish with the prosciutto pieces, then sprinkle with fresh dill, if using, and lemon juice. Season with salt and black pepper. Serve hot.

Makes 4 servings

japanese braised vegetables

see variations page 231

Lightly cooked vegetables are given an intense, bright flavor using Japanese-style sauces.

1 tsp. canola oil
1/2 tsp. sesame oil
2 tsp. fresh ginger, shredded
8 oz. broccolini
8 oz. Chinese cabbage, shredded
1 tsp. toasted sesame seeds, to serve

sauce
3 tbsp. brown miso paste
1 tsp. brown sugar
2 tbsp. white wine vinegar
1 tbsp. light soy sauce
2 tbsp. water
1 red chile, seeded and finely chopped

In a large saucepan, heat the canola and sesame oils. Pool the oils onto one side of the pan and add the ginger to cook for 1 minute. Add the vegetables and stir-fry for 1 minute. Add sufficient water to cover the base of the pan by 1/2 inch, cover, and cook for about 5 minutes, until the vegetables are tender-crisp. Drain.

Meanwhile, make the sauce by stirring all the ingredients together. Pour sauce over the cooked vegetables and toss. Sprinkle with the sesame seeds to serve.

Makes 4 servings

balsamic roasted beets

see variations page 232

Beets are colorful and exciting to eat, especially when their sweetness is balanced by the acidity of vinegar. They work particularly well alongside oily fish such as mackerel or with a piece of beef. If you buy beets with greens, wash and use them in a salad.

4 medium beets
3 tbsp. balsamic vinegar
1 tsp. fresh thyme or rosemary, finely chopped
salt

Preheat oven to 400°F.

Wash the beets but do not peel, trim the stems but do not remove — the skin needs to remain intact. Wrap each one in a piece of aluminum foil and seal tightly. Bake for 45 minutes, or until tender when pierced with a thin, sharp knife.

When just cool enough to handle, unwrap the packages and slip the skins off the beets (wear rubber gloves for this process or you will stain your hands). Slice the beets and toss in the balsamic vinegar and thyme. Season with a little salt and serve warm or cold.

Makes 4 servings

orange braised belgian endive

see variations page 233

Endive is one of those overlooked vegetables that brings so much flavor to a simple meal. It has a slight bitterness, so it needs just a little sweetening to bring out its full glory. For a special occasion, add the juniper berries.

4 Belgian endive heads
1 tbsp. canola oil
2 tsp. sugar-free maple syrup
10 juniper berries, crushed (optional)

1/3 cup orange juice
1/3 cup water
salt and black pepper

Preheat oven to 350°F.

Slice the endives in half lengthwise. Put the oil in an ovenproof skillet sufficiently large to take the endives snugly in a single layer. Drizzle skillet with maple syrup and drop in the juniper berries, if using. Put the endives in the dish, cut-side down, and pour in the orange juice and water. Season with salt and pepper.

Bake the endives, uncovered, for about 30 minutes, until tender when pierced with a thin, sharp knife. Move them to a warmed serving dish and keep warm. Bring the liquid in the skillet to a boil and cook for 1–2 minutes to reduce to a syrupy sauce. Pour sauce over the endives and serve.

Makes 4 servings

grilled corn with chipotle butter

see variations page 234

Grilled corn goes perfectly with a grilled lean steak or chicken breast. It makes a tasty light meal in itself too.

4 ears corn, husks and silk removed
1 1/2 tbsp. reduced-fat butter
2 tsp. lime juice

1 tsp. adobo sauce from can of chipotles
lemon salt or freshly ground salt,
    to serve

Put the corn in cold water to soak for 10 minutes. Drain and wipe of excess water, then put the corn on a hot grill. Close the cover and grill for 15–20 minutes, turning every 5 minutes. The cobs should be lightly charred and the kernels should feel tender when pieced with a pointed knife. The corn could also be oven-broiled, if preferred.

Meanwhile, gently melt the butter in a small saucepan and cook until it just begins to brown. Stir in the lime juice and adobo sauce. Drizzle the chipotle butter over the corn and serve with the salt.

Makes 4 servings

lemon & herb bulgur pilaf

see variations page 235

This pilaf benefits from the nutty flavor of the bulgur contrasting with the fresh flavor of the herbs. Served warm, it is great with almost any meat or poultry dish. Served cold, it makes a tasty side salad. It goes well with tzatziki (page 54).

2 tbsp. canola oil or low-fat
   cooking spray
3 medium onions, sliced
2 carrots, finely chopped
3 celery stalks, finely chopped
1 1/2 cups bulgur wheat
1/4 tsp. ground allspice
1/4 tsp. ground cinnamon

2 bay leaves
2 cups water
2 long strips lemon zest
salt and black pepper
1/4 cup fresh dill, chopped
1/4 cup fresh mint, chopped
1/4 cup fresh flat-leaf parsley, chopped
juice of 1 lemon

Heat the oil or spray in a skillet or saucepan with a tight-fitting lid. Add the onions, cook for 10 minutes, stirring occasionally, until golden brown. Add the carrot and celery and cook for 2 minutes. Add the bulgur, allspice, cinnamon, and bay leaves, and cook for 1 minute, stirring, so the bulgur is toasted with the oil.

Pour in the water and lemon zest, then season with salt and pepper. Bring to a boil, cover, and simmer over low heat for 10 minutes. Remove from the heat and let sit without stirring for 5 more minutes. Remove the bay leaves and lemon zest. Fluff up the bulgur with a fork, then stir in the dill, mint, and parsley with lemon juice to taste.

Makes 6 servings

variations

spaghetti squash with parmesan

see base recipe page 211

spaghetti squash with tomatoes & basil
Prepare the spaghetti squash, omitting sage. To the cooked garlic add the
chopped flesh of 4 peeled and seeded tomatoes. Cook for 3 minutes to heat
through. Add the squash, 1/4 cup shredded fresh basil, and the Parmesan.

cabbage fettuccine (pictured)
For cabbage pasta alternative: Thinly slice 1 white cabbage. Cook in a pan of
slightly salted water for about 5 minutes, until tender-crisp. Drain well and
serve with tomato-based pasta sauce or bolognese.

cauliflower orzo
For cauliflower pasta or rice: Break 1 head cauliflower into flowerets. Work
in batches, using a food processor, chop into rice-size pieces. Microwave,
covered, without adding any water, for about 5 minutes, stirring twice.

leek lasagna
To use leeks as lasagna noodles: Trim 2 large leeks to make them the same
length as the lasagna dish. Cut lengthwise through to the center to open
out flat. Remove small inner layers and reserve for another dish. Cook leeks
for 5 minutes in a large pan of boiling water until tender (undercooked leeks
are difficult to cut). Refresh in cold water and dry on kitchen towels.

variations

fennel & pepper bake

see base recipe page 212

baked fennel with beans

Follow the basic recipe, adding 1 (15-ounce) can white beans with
the tomatoes. Before baking, sprinkle 3/4 cup fresh bread crumbs and
2 tablespoons Parmesan cheese over the dish.

fennel & pepper tart

Prepare the basic recipe, omitting the canned tomatoes. Prepare a phyllo
tart base (page 180). Slice 2 large tomatoes and lay onto the pastry, top
with the onion and pepper mixture, and then with the fennel. Sprinkle
with 3 tablespoons Parmesan cheese and spray lightly with olive oil spray.
Bake at 400°F for 15–20 minutes. Drizzle with lemon juice, to serve.

leek & pepper bake

Prepare the basic recipe, omitting the fennel and onion. Instead lightly
cook 4 sliced medium leeks in the oil and continue as directed.

jerusalem artichoke bake

Prepare the basic recipe, replacing the fennel with 1 pound scrubbed
Jerusalem artichokes, cooked until just tender (about 20 minutes). Drain,
cool, and slice into quarters lengthwise.

variations

parmesan roasted brussels sprouts

see base recipe page 214

pecan roasted brussels sprouts
Follow the basic recipe, adding 1/4 cup pecan pieces 5 minutes before the sprouts are cooked.

parmesan roasted cauliflower
Follow the basic recipe, replacing Brussels sprouts with 1 small head of cauliflower, broken into flowerets. Cooking time will be about 30 minutes.

roasted brussels sprouts with chestnuts
Follow the basic recipe, omitting Parmesan and bread crumbs. Add 1 cup precooked chestnuts (jarred are fine) and 8 ounces small peeled shallots to the Brussels sprouts. Increase olive oil by 1 teaspoon. Cook as directed. Season with 1/2 teaspoon crushed red pepper flakes, black pepper, and a little extra salt, if needed.

roasted brussels sprouts with curry spices
Follow the basic recipe, omitting Parmesan and bread crumbs and using lemon zest instead of orange. Toss the Brussels sprouts with 1 teaspoon each of lightly crushed cumin and coriander seeds, 1 teaspoon ground garam masala, and 1/2 teaspoon each of mustard seeds and crushed red pepper flakes. Serve drizzled with lemon juice. This works well with cauliflower too.

skinnier garlicky mashed potatoes

see base recipe page 215

garlicky cauliflower potato mash
Follow the basic recipe, using 1 pound potatoes and 1/2 pound cauliflower flowerets, boiled and mashed together.

garlicky celeriac & potato mash
Follow the basic recipe, using 12 ounces each of potatoes and peeled and chopped celeriac, boiled and mashed together. Use parsley instead of chives.

roasted vegetable bake
Prepare the basic recipe. Prepare roasted vegetables (page 112), put in an ovenproof dish, and top with the potatoes. Sprinkle with 1 ounce shredded low-fat cheddar cheese and bake at 375°F for 25 minutes, until the cheese is golden.

mustard mashed potatoes
Prepare the mashed recipe, omitting the garlic and adding 2–3 tablespoons grainy mustard, to taste, with the chives.

variations

steamed cabbage with prosciutto & lemon

see base recipe page 217

steamed cabbage with soy & sesame
Follow the basic recipe, omitting prosciutto, dill, and lemon juice. Toss the
cooked cabbage with 2 tablespoons light soy sauce, 1/2 teaspoon chili oil,
and 2 teaspoons toasted sesame seeds.

steamed cabbage with spicy seeds
Prepare the basic recipe, omitting prosciutto, dill, and lemon juice. Combine
1/4 teaspoon each of caraway seeds, celery seeds, crushed red pepper flakes,
cumin seeds, black mustard seeds, and cracked black pepper. Dry-fry for
1 minute, stirring. Toss cooked cabbage in 1 tablespoon each of chicken
broth and canola oil, and then toss with seeds.

steamed cabbage wedges
Follow the basic recipe, but instead of shredding cabbage, cut the half
cabbage into 4 wedges, then cut out the central core keeping the wedges
intact. Sprinkle with dried dill, if using. Steam for 6 minutes, turn carefully,
and steam for another 6 minutes, or until tender. Finish as directed.

slow-cooked cabbage with prosciutto
Prepare the prosciutto. Put cabbage in a pan, cover tightly and cook for 1 hour
over very low heat, turning occasionally. If cabbage is still watery, remove the
lid to allow water to evaporate; cook for 2 more minute. Finsh as directed.

japanese braised vegetables

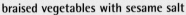

see base recipe page 218

braised vegetables with sesame salt
Prepare the vegetables, omitting the sauce. Toast 1/4 cup sesame seeds in a dry skillet until golden; cool. Add 1/4 teaspoon salt and cook, stirring until just beginning to brown; cool. Crush the sesame and salt with a pestle and mortar until most of the seeds are broken up, or lightly process in a small blender. Sprinkle over vegetables.

japanese vegetable salad
Prepare the vegetables, omitting the sauce and sesame seeds. Make a dressing from 1/2 cup dashi or chicken broth, 1 tablespoon light soy sauce, and 1 tablespoon mirin or sweet sherry. Pour over the vegetables, let sit for at least 1 hour. Sprinkle with bonito flakes or dried seaweed flakes.

japanese braised spinach
Cook the ginger in the oils. Take 1 pound washed spinach. Add a third of the spinach to pan; when it wilts, add another third, followed by the last third. Toss, cover, and steam in the water clinging to the leaves for 3–5 minutes, until the spinach is just cooked; drain. Serve with the basic sauce.

vegetables with cashews & oyster sauce
Prepare the basic recipe, omitting the sauce. Toast 1/2 cup raw cashews in a skillet until golden. Add to the drained vegetables and toss with 2–3 tablespoons oyster sauce.

variations

balsamic roasted beets

see base recipe page 219

beets with sour cream dressing
Cook and slice the beets as directed. Toss with 1 teaspoon each of honey
and balsamic vinegar and season with salt. Add 1/2 cup non-fat sour cream
and 2 tablespoons chopped fresh dill.

beet & goat cheese salad
Follow the basic recipe. Cool to room temperature. Toss with 2 cups arugula
and 1/4 cup toasted walnuts and put on plates. Cut 2 (4-ounce) rolls of goat
cheese into 1/4-inch slices and broil for several minutes until browning at the
edges. Put on top of the salad to serve.

beets with orange balsamic glaze
Cook and slice the beets. Mix 3 tablespoons orange juice and 1 teaspoon
orange zest with the vinegar. If serving warm, put the mixture in the
microwave to warm for 20 seconds before adding to beets.

spiced beets
Cook and slice the beets. In a skillet, dry-roast 1/2 teaspoon each of ground
cumin, ground coriander, and black mustard seeds, plus 1/4 teaspoon
cayenne pepper, until the seeds begin to pop. Stir in beets, 2 tablespoons
lemon juice, and 2 teaspoons honey; toss to heat through and evenly coat.
Season with salt and black pepper and serve with a little non-fat yogurt.

orange braised endive

see base recipe page 220

cider braised endive
Prepare the basic recipe, omitting orange juice and water and using 2/3 cup hard cider. Omit juniper berries and add 1/3 teaspoon dried thyme.

braised endive with blue cheese
Prepare the basic recipe, omitting orange juice and water and using 2/3 cup chicken or vegetable broth. Cook the endive for 20 minutes, remove from oven, crumble 2 ounces low-fat blue cheese over the top, and cook another 10 minutes.

orange braised leeks
Replace the basic recipe, replacing endive with 4 medium leeks, trimmed to the light green part and cut in half lengthwise.

orange braised carrots with rosemary
Prepare the basic recipe, replacing the endive with 1 1/2 pounds trimmed and scrubbed baby carrots. Cut carrots in half lengthwise if chunky and arrange in a single layer (or at most a double layer) in an ovenproof dish. Add 2 sprigs rosemary, cover with foil, and bake at 400°F for about 30 minutes until tender. Remove the foil and cook for another 10 minutes until the edges begin turning dark brown.

variations

grilled corn with chipotle butter

see base recipe page 223

grilled corn with cilantro & chile pesto
Cook the corn as directed, omitting butter. Make 4 tablespoons cilantro and pumpkin seed pesto (page 178), add 1 seeded and finely chopped red chile. Serve drizzled over the corn cobs.

mexican street corn
Cook the corn as directed, omitting butter. Combine 4 tablespoons low-fat mayonnaise with 1 teaspoon each of chili powder and garlic salt; season with black pepper. Crumble in 1/4 cup crumbled Cotija cheese or shredded Parmesan. Serve drizzled over the corn with a wedge of lime.

grilled corn salsa
Cook the corn as directed, omitting butter. Cool, then strip the kernels from the cobs. Combine kernels with 1/2 cup chopped red bell pepper, 1/2 chopped red onion, 1–2 chopped jarred jalapeño peppers, 1/2 cup halved cherry tomatoes, 2 tablespoons each lime juice and chopped fresh cilantro, and 1/2 teaspoon each ground cumin, garlic salt, and pepper. Let sit for 1 hour at room temperature before serving.

grilled corn with yogurt & chives
Cook the sweetcorn omitting butter. To serve: combine 1/2 cup non-fat yogurt with 2 tablespoons snipped chives, salt, and paprika to taste.

variations

lemon & herb bulgur pilaf

see base recipe page 224

lemon & herb bulgur pumpkin pilaf
Follow the basic recipe, omitting carrots and celery and adding 2 cups
peeled, seeded pumpkin flesh, cut into 1/4-inch pieces.

lemon & herb couscous pilaf
Follow the basic recipe, using 1 1/2 cups pearl couscous (also called Israeli
couscous) instead of bulgur wheat. Bring to a boil, then simmer for about
12 minutes until just tender and the water evaporated.

lemon & herb brown rice pilaf
Follow the basic recipe, using 1 cup long-grain brown rice (not instant)
instead of bulgur wheat. Use 2 1/2 cups vegetable or chicken broth instead
of water, bring to a boil, cover, then simmer for about 45 minutes, until
tender. Uncover and let rice stand for 5 minutes before proceeding.

lemon & herb bulgur shrimp pilaf
Follow the basic recipe, adding 1 pound cooked medium shrimp with the
herbs. Let rest in a warm place for 3 minutes or until the shrimp are
heated through.

desserts

Here is a gorgeous collection of sin-free treats.

Some recipes are based on the good, rich flavor

of fresh fruit; some exploit the magical low-fat

properties of a well-deployed egg white; and

others take advantage of the low-fat and indeed

the non-fat cream cheeses, yogurts, and sour

creams now available. Even tofu makes a showing

as a secret ingredient.

roasted mangoes with ginger yogurt

see variations page 250

The divine taste of beautiful fresh fruit is intensified by roasting so that the sugars caramelize and the flavor bursts out. This method works well for many fruits, such as peaches, plums, pears, apples, pineapple, and oranges.

2 mangoes
4 teaspoons sugar-free maple syrup

ginger yogurt
1 1/2 cups non-fat yogurt, preferably Greek-style

1/3 cup crystalized ginger, chopped
1–2 tbsp. brown sugar or equivalent
  in sugar substitute
1 tsp. lemon juice

Preheat broiler to medium.

Using a sharp knife, slice the mangoes lengthwise and cut carefully around the pit. Score the flesh into 1/2-inch cubes, taking care not to cut through the skin. Using the thumbs, gently invert the mango halves to reveal the fleshy cubes. Put skin-side down on a foil-lined broiler pan. Drizzle with the maple syrup and broil for 3–5 minutes, until the flesh is soft and the tops are just beginning to catch at the edges.

Meanwhile soak the crystallized ginger in boiling water for 5 minutes to remove the sugar. Drain, cool, and chop finely in a small bowl, combine with yogurt, brown sugar, and lemon juice, adjusting to taste. Serve with the mango.

Makes 4 servings

berry-mango parfait

see variations page 251

Very simple, yet satisfying, these little desserts look extremely attractive and make a delicious end to a meal. Greek yogurt is used because of its extra body, but it does have a few more calories than some other plain yogurts, so the choice is yours. If you have a sweet tooth, you may want to add a little sugar or sweetener to the berries.

1/2 cup fat-free, low-sugar granola or
   6 crumbled amaretti cookies
2 cups non-fat Greek yogurt

2 cups mixed berries (blueberries, raspberries, sliced strawberries)
flesh of 1 ripe mango, puréed

Put the granola or crumbled cookies in the base of 4 sundae dishes or large wineglasses. Layer the yogurt, berries, and mango purée, finishing with a few berries on the top.

Makes 4 servings

light chocolate mousse

see variations page 252

Don't be put off by the ingredients in this mousse. If you didn't know a major constituent was silken tofu, you would never be able to tell. This recipe contains uncooked egg whites, which lighten the mousse but are unsuitable for those with compromised immune systems. There is an egg white-free variation.

1 (12-oz.) package silken tofu, room
    temperature, drained
2/3 cup semisweet chocolate chips
1/2 cup cocoa powder
3 tbsp. sugar-free maple syrup
1 tsp. vanilla extract

few drops almond extract or 2 tbsp. almond
    liqueur or brandy
2 egg whites
fruit such as kiwi slices, raspberries, or cherries,
    to garnish

Beat the tofu by hand or in a food processor until smooth.

In a double boiler, melt the chocolate chips, stirring frequently until smooth. Add to the tofu with the cocoa powder, maple syrup, vanilla, and almond extract or liqueur. Beat by hand to combine.

Beat the egg whites until firm peaks form. Fold about one third of the egg white mixture into the chocolate mixture to lighten. Using a large metal spoon, fold half of the resulting mixture into the stiff egg whites. When combined, carefully fold in the remaining chocolate mixture. Spoon the mixture into a large serving bowl. Refrigerate until required, then garnish with fruit.

Makes 6–8 servings

strawberry & lemon mini soufflés

see variations page 253

These little soufflés are intense in flavor and amazingly light and almost fat-free.

1 tbsp. superfine sugar, to dust	pinch salt	1 tsp. vanilla extract
8 oz. strawberries	1/4 cup superfine sugar or equivalent in sugar substitute	1 tsp. grated lemon zest
5 egg whites		2 tbsp. lemon juice
		confectioners' sugar, to serve

Preheat the oven to 350°F. Use low-fat spray to grease 4 ramekins or mini soufflé dishes with a 1 1/4-cup capacity. Dust the inside with superfine sugar, tapping out any excess.

Purée the strawberries in a food processor, then pour into a non-metallic sieve and place over a bowl to drain off excess liquid. Put strawberry purée into a new bowl.

In a clean, dry bowl, beat the egg whites and salt with an electric mixer until they form soft peaks. With the mixer running, slowly add the sugar and continue to beat until the egg whites form stiff peaks. Add the vanilla and lemon zest, and beat to combine. Fold about one quarter of the egg white mixture into the strawberry mixture to lighten. Using a large metal spoon, fold in half the remaining egg whites, then repeat. Spoon the mixture into the prepared dishes, taking care to spread the mixture to the sides of the dishes; flatten the tops.

Transfer the ramekins to a baking sheet and bake in the oven for about 10–12 minutes, until risen and lightly browned. Do not open the oven door while the soufflés are cooking. Dust with confectioners' sugar and serve immediately.

Makes 4 servings

frozen cherry yogurt

see variations page 254

This frozen yogurt is very quick and easy to make and its bright flavor makes a perfect end to a meal. For special occasions, you can add a little liqueur to add a kick.

2 cups pitted fresh cherries, frozen cherries,
   or jarred cherries in natural juices
1/4 cup cherry juice or cranberry juice
1 1/4 cups non-fat Greek yogurt

1 tsp. lime zest
2 tbsp. honey or sugar-free maple syrup,
   or to taste
2 tbsp. kirsch or amaretto liqueur (optional)

Put the cherries and juice in a blender and process until smooth. Add the yogurt, lime zest, and honey or maple syrup. Process until smooth.

Transfer to an ice-cream maker and churn to freeze. Alternatively, put in a wide plastic container and freeze for 2 hours, stirring with a fork to break up the ice crystals as they form around the edges. Repeat, then transfer to the food processor and process until smooth. Add the kirsch or amaretto, if using.

Turn the frozen yogurt into a plastic container and keep frozen until 20–30 minutes before serving. Let stand at room temperature to facilitate scooping, but if you used liqueur, you can serve direct from the freezer.

Makes 6 servings

raspberry cheesecake

see variations page 255

This is not a really low-calorie dessert, but it does contain under two-thirds of the calories of its regular counterpart. The base is thinner and contains less fat, the cheese is low-fat, and you can use a sugar substitute. Using raspberries in the cheesecake makes it attractive and means that a topping is not necessary. But all this doesn't mean you can justify a giant slice!

3 tbsp. low-fat butter or spread
1 cup graham cracker crumbs
1 1/4 lb. low-fat soft cream cheese,
    room temperature
1/4 cup superfine sugar, or equivalent in sugar
    substitute
3 tbsp. cornstarch

grated zest of 1 lemon
1 tbsp. lemon juice
1 tsp. vanilla extract
2 eggs, lightly beaten
1 egg white
1/2 cup fresh or frozen (do not defrost)
    raspberries

Preheat oven to 350°F.

Line a 9-inch springform pan with parchment paper. Combine the butter and graham cracker crumbs in a bowl, then press into the base of the baking pan. Bake for 10 minutes.

In a clean bowl, beat the cream cheese until soft. Gently stir in the sugar and cornstarch, followed by the lemon zest, lemon juice, vanilla, eggs, and egg whites. Do not overbeat. Pour the filling over the base. Push the raspberries into the surface of the cheesecake, distributing them evenly.

Return to the oven for 15 minutes. Reduce the heat to 225°F. Bake for an additional 25 minutes or until the outside edges of the cheesecake are firm but the center is still quite wobbly. Turn off the oven and leave the cheesecake in the oven with the door closed for 2 hours. Let cool, refrigerate until an hour before serving, then bring to room temperature to serve.

Makes 10 slices

raspberry cloud

see variations page 256

This delicious light mousse is perfect after a rich meal.

2 1/4 cups frozen raspberries
1 (3-oz.) package raspberry-flavored
   sugar-free gelatin

2 egg whites
2 tbsp. superfine sugar or sweetener
fresh mint leaves, to decorate

Reserve 1/4 cup raspberries for decoration. Crush the remaining raspberries while still frozen.

Make the gelatin using 2/3 cup boiling water. Add the raspberries, then put bowl in the refrigerator until almost set.

Beat the egg whites with the sugar until stiff but not dry. Fold into the raspberry gelatin mixture. Transfer to a glass serving bowl or put in individual dishes and return to the refrigerator to set thoroughly. Decorate with reserved raspberries and mint leaves.

Makes 6 servings

sharp lemon tart

see variations page 257

Calories have been slashed from this classic recipe by using the low-fat crust (page 19), cutting the number of egg yolks, and being economical with the sugar. Using brown sugar adds a richness to compensate for fewer egg yolks. To lose more calories, use powdered egg substitute and sugar substitute. You may wish to make only partial substitutions, though, to keep that home-cooked flavor.

1 recipe low-fat pastry (page 19)
3 tbsp. half-fat butter, melted
2 eggs
3 tbsp. brown sugar

3 tbsp. sugar or half equivalent in sugar substitute
juice and zest of 2 lemons
confectioners' sugar (optional)

Preheat oven to 375°F.

Use the pastry to line an 8-inch pie plate, trim, and flute. Chill. Line the pastry with parchment paper and pie weights and bake blind for 10 minutes, remove the pie weights and paper, and cook for a further 3 minutes to dry out base. Reduce the oven temperature to 300°F.

Make the filling by mixing the butter, eggs, and both sugars in a heatproof bowl over a pan of simmering water, stirring until the sugar has melted. Add the lemon zest and juice. Pour through a sieve into the warm pie crust. Bake for 25–30 minutes until just firm to touch. Serve at room temperature, dusted with confectioners' sugar if desired.

Makes 5 servings

variations

roasted mangoes with ginger yogurt

see base recipe page 237

foil-roasted barbecue oranges with ginger yogurt
Peel and segment 4 oranges. Combine with 2 tablespoons sugar-free maple
syrup and 1 teaspoon apple pie spice. Divide mixture between 4 pieces of
foil and wrap tightly. Barbecue over a medium heat for 15–20 minutes.

roasted apples & pears with ginger yogurt
Peel, core, and chop 2 apples and 2 pears, put in a baking pan, and toss with
1 tablespoon lemon juice to prevent discoloration. Add 2–3 tablespoons brown
sugar or the equivalent in sugar substitute, and 1/2 teaspoon cinnamon.
Toss again. Roast at 425°F for 25 minutes until tender and golden.

roasted piña colada
Cut 1 pineapple into 1/2-inch-thick slices and broil, drizzled with maple
syrup, on a foil-lined pan for 10–15 minutes per side. Serve with low fat
coconut yogurt. Top with a maraschino or candied cherry.

grilled balsamic figs with ginger yogurt
Halve 8 large or 12 small ripe figs lengthwise. Put figs cut-side down on a
heatproof dish and brush their backs with a little oil. Turn over and brush
with good balsamic vinegar. Sprinkle with 2 tablespoons brown sugar or
sugar substitute. Broil for 5–8 minutes, until the sugar begins to caramelize.

berry-mango parfait

see base recipe page 238

caramelized apple parfait
Follow the basic recipe, omitting mango and berries. Heat 1 tablespoon low-fat butter or spread. Slice 2 Granny Smith apples and gently cook with 2 tablespoons sugar-free maple syrup and 1 teaspoon apple pie spice, turning occasionally until soft; cool. Layer with yogurt and granola or amaretti crumbs.

berry yogurt swirl
Omit mango. In a small saucepan, combine the berries with 2 tablespoons lemon juice, 1 teaspoon lemon zest, and 2 tablespoons brown sugar or sugar substitute. Stir over medium heat until the berries begin to soften, about 3 minutes. Remove from the heat, cool, then chill. Just before serving, swirl the berries into the yogurt, keeping stirring to a minimum to create a mottled effect. Serve immediately on top of granola in glass dishes.

berry yogurt semifreddo
Follow the recipe above for berry yogurt swirl. Transfer the berry–yogurt mixture to a plastic container and freeze until almost set. Serve in scoops in glasses on top of the granola.

mango & kiwi chocolate parfait
Follow basic recipe, replacing the berries with 3 kiwi fruits and the plain yogurt with non-fat chocolate yogurt.

light chocolate mousse

see base recipe page 240

light chocolate & berry mousse

Follow the basic recipe, adding 2 cups mixed berries, sweetened to taste with sugar-free maple syrup, to the base of the serving bowl.

mocha mousse

Follow the basic recipe, but omit almond extract and use just 1/2 teaspoon vanilla. Add 2 tablespoons instant coffee granules with the cocoa powder.

rich chocolate mousse

Follow the basic recipe, but omit the egg whites. This makes a very rich mousse. Distribute between 4–6 serving bowls. Suitable for vegans and those with low immunity.

black & white chocolate mousse

Divide the beaten tofu between 2 bowls. In the first bowl, follow the basic instructions but use half of the listed ingredients. To the second bowl, add 3/4 cup white chocolate chips, which have been melted over a double boiler, and 1/2 teaspoon vanilla extract. Finish as directed, dividing the beaten egg whites between the bowls. Put in layers in tall glasses.

variations

strawberry & lemon mini soufflés

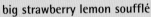

see base recipe page 241

big strawberry lemon soufflé

Prepare a large soufflé dish with a 5-cup capacity as directed. Make the soufflé mixture following the basic instructions, transfer to the large soufflé dish, and bake for about 30 minutes until well risen and golden brown. Serve immediately.

strawberry & chocolate soufflé

Follow the basic recipe, omitting lemon juice and zest. Add 2 tablespoons sifted cocoa powder with the vanilla.

apricot soufflé

Follow the basic recipe, replacing strawberries with an apricot purée. In a covered saucepan, cook 1 cup dried apricots, 1 cup water, and 1/3 cup sugar or equivalent in sugar substitute. While still warm, purée, pass through a non-metallic sieve, and cool to room temperature before proceeding.

raspberry & orange soufflé

Follow the basic recipe, using raspberries instead of strawberries and orange zest and juice or orange-flavored liqueur instead of lemon juice.

variations

frozen cherry yogurt

see base recipe page 243

cherry & almond smoothie
Follow the basic recipe. Put 2 scoops frozen cherry yogurt in a blender
with 1 cup almond milk and a few drops almond extract. Blend until smooth,
then sweeten to taste with 2–3 teaspoons sugar-free maple syrup.

cherry sorbet
Follow the basic recipe, omitting yogurt and adding 2 lightly beaten
egg whites.

frozen mandarin chocolate chip yogurt
Follow the basic recipe, using 1 (15-ounce) can mandarin oranges in
natural juice instead of cherries and cherry or cranberry juice. Use orange
zest in place of lime zest. Add 1/2 cup mini semisweet chocolate chips to
the frozen yogurt just before transferring it to the plastic container.

coconut–cherry frozen yogurt
Follow the basic recipe, but roughly chop the cherries and omit the lime
zest. With the yogurt, add 1 (15-ounce) can low-fat coconut milk and
1/2 teaspoon coconut extract or 1 tablespoon coconut rum.

variations

raspberry cheesecake

see base recipe page 244

marble chocolate cheesecake
Follow the basic recipe, omitting raspberries. Melt and cool 1/4 cup semisweet chocolate chips. Add 1 cup cheesecake filling to the chocolate and mix well. Pour chocolate mixture over the plain cheesecake mixture and, using a knife, cut it through to create a rough marbled effect. Carefully pour over the base and bake as directed.

ginger & raspberry cheesecake
Follow the basic recipe, adding 1 teaspoon ground ginger to the butter before mixing with the cookie crumbs. Also add 4 finely chopped pieces preserved ginger to the filling.

strawberry cheesecake
Follow the basic recipe, omitting raspberries and adding 1 cup chopped strawberries to the filling. Serve topped with a few strawberries glazed with sugar-free strawberry preserves.

citrus cheesecake
Follow the basic recipe, omitting raspberries and adding 2 teaspoons orange zest and 1/2 teaspoon lime zest to the filling. Serve topped with a thin layer (about 2/3 cup) of sugar-free orange marmalade thinned with 2 teaspoons orange juice.

raspberry cloud

see base recipe page 247

citrus cloud

Follow the basic recipe, using lemon-flavored gelatin. Peel 3 medium oranges and with a sharp knife, slice the fresh from the membranes; roughly chop and use instead of the raspberries.

lime, coconut & pineapple cloud

Follow the basic recipe, using lime-flavored gelatin. Instead of raspberries, use 1 3/4 cups crushed pineapple, drained of excess juice and 1/2 cup shredded coconut.

strawberry passion fruit cloud

Follow the basic recipe, using strawberry gelatin. Omit raspberries and use 1 1/4 cup fresh, frozen, or canned sliced strawberries and 1 cup passion fruit pulp.

raspberry cloud pie

Make the raspberry cloud as directed. Grease an 8-inch soufflé dish with low-fat spray and line the base and sides with ladyfingers. Sprinkle dish with 1 cup mixed berries. Top with raspberry cloud (you will have more than you need). Combine 3/4 cup non-fat sour cream, 1/2 teaspoon vanilla, and 1–2 tablespoons sugar or sugar substitute to taste. Spread over top of pie. Serve chilled.

sharp lemon tart

see base recipe page 248

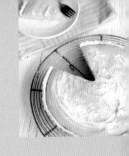

key lime tart

Follow the basic recipe for the pie crust, adding 2 tablespoons cocoa powder
with the flour. Prepare the filling, using Key limes (or limes) instead of lemons.
Melt 2 squares dark chocolate (or diabetic dark chocolate) in a bowl over a
double boiler. When the pie has cooled, drizzle the top with melted chocolate.

blood orange tart

Follow the basic recipe, using the zest and juice of 2 blood oranges plus
2 tablespoons lemon juice in place of the lemons.

creamy lemon tart

Follow the basic recipe. When the filling is made, sieve the egg mixture into
a clean bowl. Beat in 3/4 cup non-fat sour cream and pour the mixture into
the warm pie crust. Cook as directed.

baking

Lots of people enjoy a slice of cake or a cookie with their coffee from time to time. The following selection uses techniques to reduce fats and sugars and, consequently, calories, so you can have your cake and eat it too. Just beware of portion size.

oatmeal chocolate chip cookies

see variations page 274

These little morsels of loveliness, in spite of being lower-calorie than your average cookie, lose nothing by way of irresistibility. For dairy-free and gluten-free cookies, see variations.

1/2 cup whole wheat flour	1/2 tsp. ground cinnamon	1/4 cup fat-free Greek yogurt or strained plain yogurt
1/2 cup all-purpose flour	1 egg	1 tsp. vanilla extract
1/2 tsp. baking soda	1 cup light brown sugar or equivalent in sugar substitute	1 1/3 cups old-fashioned oats
1/2 tsp. baking powder	2 tbsp. canola oil	3/4 cup chocolate chips
1/2 tsp. salt		

Preheat the oven to 350°F. Line 2 cookie sheets with parchment paper.

In a large bowl, sift together the flours, baking soda, baking powder, salt, and cinnamon.

In a small bowl, lightly beat the egg, then beat in the sugar, oil, yogurt, and vanilla. Stir into the dry ingredients until just combined. Stir in the oats and chocolate chips.

Drop rounded teaspoons of the dough onto the baking sheets, pressing down lightly with the back of a spoon. Bake for about 10 minutes until golden brown. The cookies will be very slightly undercooked in the middle, which results in a moist, chewy cookie. Continue to cook for a couple more minutes for a crisper cookie. Let cookies cool on the sheets for 5 minutes, then transfer them to wire racks to cool completely.

Makes 40 small cookies

strawberry shortcake

see variations page 275

You can still eat strawberry shortcake with this lower-calorie recipe. By flavoring the strawberries with balsamic vinegar, the sugar is reduced; by replacing the cream with fat-free vanilla yogurt, the fat is reduced; and by using only one layer of shortcake, the calories are reduced. You do still need to use proper butter, as the water in the low-fat options compromise the finished shortcake.

strawberries
1 lb. strawberries, hulled and
  quartered
1 tbsp. sugar or equivalent in
  sugar substitute
1 tbsp. balsamic vinegar

shortcake
1 cup all-purpose flour
2 tsp. sugar or equivalent in
  sugar substitute
1 1/4 tsp. baking powder
pinch baking soda
pinch salt
2 tbsp. cold butter

1 egg
1/3 cup low-fat buttermilk
1 tbsp. 1% milk

topping
1 cup fat-free vanilla yogurt
1 tsp. orange zest

Preheat oven to 425°F. Grease an 8-inch round baking pan with low-fat cooking spray.

Combine the strawberries, 1 tablespoon sugar, and balsamic vinegar in a bowl. Set aside.

To make the shortcake, stir together the flour, sugar, baking powder, and baking soda, and salt in a large bowl. Cut in the butter until the mixture resembles bread crumbs. In a small bowl, beat together egg and buttermilk. Add to the dry ingredients all at once and stir until just combined. Don't worry if the mixture is still a bit lumpy. Using lightly floured hands, press the mixture into the prepared pan, brush with 1% milk to glaze, and bake for

12-15 minutes until risen and golden brown. Cool in the pan for 5 minutes, then transfer to a wire rack to cool completely.

To serve, combine the yogurt and orange zest, spread over the shortcake, and top with the strawberries.

Makes 8 servings

angel food cake
with blackberry coulis

see variations page 276

This cake is as low in calories as cake can possibly be.

12 egg whites
1 1/4 tsp. cream of tartar
1 1/2 cups superfine sugar or
    equivalent in sugar
    substitute

1 tsp. vanilla extract
grated zest of 1 lemon
1 cup sifted cake flour
powdered sugar or substitute
    to dust (optional)

blackberry coulis
3 cups fresh blackberries
1/4 cup orange juice
3 tbsp. sugar-free maple
    syrup, or to taste

Preheat the oven to 350°F. Have ready a Bundt pan pan or 10-inch tube pan, ungreased.

Put the egg whites one at a time into a large, grease-free, dry bowl. Beat with an electric mixer until frothy, add the cream of tartar, and beat until soft peaks form. Slowly add the sugar, vanilla, and lemon zest. Continue to beat until stiff peaks form and eggs are glossy.

Sift one third of the flour into the beaten egg whites and fold in very gently with a large metal spoon; repeat in two more additions. Pour the batter into the pan. Run a knife through the batter to remove any air pockets and smooth the top gently. Bake for 35–40 minutes, until the top is golden brown and a skewer inserted into the center comes out clean. Let cool completely. Loosen edges and invert onto a wire rack. Dust with a little powdered sugar.

Purée 2 cups blackberries with the orange juice. Press through a non-metallic sieve, then sweeten to taste with maple syrup. Stir in the remaining berries. Serve with the cake.
Makes 12–16 servings

skinny vanilla raspberry cupcakes

see variations page 277

These cupcakes are made with low-fat spread to reduce calories, but they don't miss out on taste — they have the intense flavor that comes from using real vanilla. Vanilla paste is a convenient and economical way to get the speckled look and vibrant flavor of fresh vanilla, but it varies by manufacturer, so check the label for to see how many teaspoons equal one fresh bean.

1/2 cup low-fat spread
1/2 cup sugar or equivalent in sugar substitute
2 eggs
scraped seeds from 1/2 vanilla bean or 1–2 tsp. vanilla paste (see note above)

1 1/4 cups flour
1 1/4 tsp. baking powder
36 fresh or frozen (not defrosted) raspberries

Preheat oven to 350°F. Line a 12-cup muffin pan with cupcake liners.

Put the spread and sugar in a mixing bowl. Beat with an electric mixer or wooden spoon for 2–3 minutes, until light and fluffy. Beat in the eggs one at a time. Stir in the vanilla seeds or paste. Sift together the flour and baking powder and fold in with a large metal spoon or spatula until combined. Spoon the mixture into the cupcake liners. Drop 3 raspberries onto the top of each cupcake.

Bake the cupcakes for 15–20 minutes, or until a toothpick inserted into the center comes out clean. Transfer onto a wire rack and cool for 5 minutes before transferring the cupcakes from the muffin pan onto a wire rack to cool completely.

Makes 12 cupcakes

zucchini cranberry bread

see variations page 278

This fruit bread, made with as little oil possible, is light and quite delicious. If you don't have low-fat sour cream on hand, use low-fat Greek yogurt.

1 cup whole wheat flour
1/2 cup cake flour
2/3 cup brown sugar or
    equivalent in sugar
    substitute
1 1/2 tsp. baking powder
3/4 tsp. baking soda

1/2 tsp. salt
1 tsp. ground cinnamon
1/4 tsp. ground nutmeg
1 egg
1 egg white
1/4 cup canola oil
1/4 cup low-fat sour cream

2 tsp. vanilla extract
grated zest and juice of
    1/2 lemon
1 1/4 cups zucchini, shredded,
    tightly packed, and
    squeezed dry
3/4 cup dried cranberries

Preheat oven to 350°F. Base line a 9x5-inch bread pan and grease with low-fat cooking spray.

In a large bowl, mix together the flours, sugar, baking powder, baking soda, salt, cinnamon, and nutmeg.

In a separate bowl, lightly beat the egg and egg white, stir in the oil, sour cream, vanilla, lemon zest, and lemon juice. Stir into the dry ingredients. Using a spatula, stir in the grated zucchini and cranberries. Pour into the prepared pan and bake for 50–60 minutes until the top is golden and a skewer inserted into the center of the cake comes out clean. Let sit for 10 minutes, then turn out to cook on a wire rack.

Makes about 10 slices

lemon roulade

see variations page 279

This is a very pretty cake and light as a feather. Do not substitute a sugar alternative in this recipe, because it acts differently than sugar and may not thicken as required to rise the cake.

roulade
3 eggs
1/3 cup sugar
3 tbsp. water
3/4 cup cake flour, sifted
1 tsp. baking powder
1/4 tsp. salt
1 tsp. lemon zest

to finish
1/2 cup low-fat cream cheese
1 cup non-fat thick lemon yogurt
3/4 cup blueberries
3/4 cup raspberries
confectioners' sugar, to dust

Preheat oven to 400°F. Base line and grease a 10 1/2-x15 1/2-inch jelly roll pan with non-fat cooking spray.

Using an electric mixer and a heatproof bowl placed over a pan of simmering water, beat the eggs and sugar until pale and creamy and thick enough to leave a trail on the surface when the whisk is lifted. This takes about 10 minutes. Whisk in the water.

Sift together the flour, baking powder, and salt, then sift half the dry mixture over the egg mixture and fold it in very lightly using a large metal spoon or spatula. Sift in the remaining flour and the lemon zest, and fold in very gently until incorporated, using the minimum number of turns. Pour the mixture into the prepared pan, tilting to spread the mixture evenly into the corners. Bake for 12–15 minutes, until well risen, lightly golden, and firm to the touch.

Let cool in pan for 5 minutes. Sprinkle a piece of parchment paper or clean dish towel all over with superfine sugar, and turn out the sponge onto it. Cut off the crusty edges with a sharp knife, then roll up the sponge jelly-roll fashion. Let cool while rolled up with the paper or towel.

For the filling, combine the cream cheese and yogurt. Carefully unroll the roulade onto the paper or dish towel and spread it with the yogurt mixture. Sprinkle with the berries. Reroll by slowly lifting the paper or dish towel. Transfer to a serving plate. Serve at once or chill until required.

Makes 8–10 slices

sicilian orange polenta cake

see variations page 280

This Italian-style cake is moist and orangey with a slightly gritty texture and a hint of cardamom that makes it quite yummy cold or warm with fat-free sour cream.

3 eggs
3/4 cup sugar or equivalent in sugar
    substitute
1/4 cup olive oil
zest of 2 oranges, preferably blood oranges
1/2 tsp. vanilla extract

seeds of 8 green cardamom pods, ground
1 cup plus 2 tbsp. polenta (yellow cornmeal)
1/2 cup all-purpose flour
1 1/2 tsp. baking powder
1/2 tsp. salt
1/4 cup orange juice

Preheat the oven to 300°F. Base-line a 9-inch loose-bottomed cake pan with baking parchment and grease with low-fat cooking spray.

With an electric mixer, beat the eggs and sugar until light and creamy, about 5 minutes. With the mixer running, slowly drizzle in the olive oil, until all the oil is combined. Add the orange zest, vanilla, and cardamom.

In separate bowl, stir together the polenta, flour, baking powder, and salt. Sift one third of this mixture over the eggs. Fold in with a large metal spoon or spatula, alternating with the orange juice, folding until just combined. Repeat with remaining flour mixture and orange juice. Pour batter into the prepared cake pan and bake for 40–45 minutes until a skewer inserted into the center comes out clean. Let cool in the pan for about 10 minutes, then turn out onto a wire rack to cool completely.

Makes 8–12 servings

pistachio & orange biscotti

see variations page 281

These extremely low-fat cookies make great gifts. They store well too, so you might want to double up the quantities while you are in baking mode.

1 cup plus 2 tbsp. all-purpose flour
1/2 cup sugar or equivalent in sugar
   substitute
3/4 tsp. baking powder
1/4 tsp. salt
1 1/2 tsp. grated orange zest

1 egg
1 tbsp. 1% milk
1 tbsp. canola oil
1 tbsp. orange juice
1/2 tsp. vanilla extract
1/2 cup unsalted pistachios

Preheat oven to 350°F. Line a cookie sheet with parchment paper or a silicone mat.

Combine the flour, sugar, baking powder, salt, and orange zest in a bowl. In a separate bowl, with a hand whisk, beat together the egg, milk, oil, orange juice, and vanilla. Slowly add the egg mixture into the dry ingredients followed by the pistachios. Mix with a wooden spoon or hands until the dough comes together, adding a little more milk if it fails to clump together.

Turn dough out onto a floured surface and, with floured hands, knead until smooth. Shape into a 3-inch-wide log. Transfer log to the prepared cookie sheet and bake for about 25 minutes until cooked through. Put on a wire rack to cool for 15 minutes. Cut the warm log into 1/2-inch slices on the diagonal using a sharp serrated knife and a gentle sawing action. Put the cookies on the cookie sheet and bake for another 15–20 minutes until quite dry but not colored. Put the cookie sheet on a wire rack to cool completely.

Makes about 24 cookies

craving for chocolate cake

see variations page 282

This cake has the rich taste of chocolate but without all the calories. It has a lovely glossy top, so it needs no frosting. Double the recipe to make a 9x13-inch pan and cook for a few minutes longer.

3/4 cup plus 2 tablespoons cake flour
2 tbsp. brown sugar
1/3 cup cocoa powder
1 tsp. coffee powder
1 1/4 tsp. baking soda
1/2 tsp. salt

1/4 cup applesauce
1 1/4 cups fat-free yogurt
1 egg
1 tsp. vanilla extract
2 egg whites
1/2 cup sugar or equivalent in sugar substitute

Preheat the oven to 350°F. Grease an 8x8-inch baking pan and base line with parchment paper.

Set out 3 bowls. In the first, combine the flour, brown sugar, cocoa and coffee powders, baking soda, and salt. In the second, beat together the applesauce, yogurt, egg, and vanilla. In the third, beat the egg whites with clean beaters until soft peaks form, add the sugar, and continue to beat until firm peaks form and the mixture is glossy.

Combine the dry ingredients and the applesauce mixture. Mix in one third of the egg white mixture. Using a large metal spoon or spatula, gently fold in the remaining egg whites in two batches until just combined. Pour into the prepared cake pan and bake for about 30 minutes until a skewer inserted into the center comes out clean. Transfer onto a wire rack and cool for 5 minutes before turning the cake out onto a wire rack and allowing to cool completely.

Makes 12 pieces

caraway oat crackers

see variations page 283

These tasty little crackers are easy to make and are a delicious accompaniment for soup, pâté, or cold meats and cheese.

1 cup whole wheat flour
1 1/2 cups old-fashioned oats
1/2 tsp. salt
1/4 tsp. black pepper

1 1/2 tbsp. caraway seeds
3 tbsp. olive or canola oil
1/2 cup boiling water

Preheat oven to 350°F. Dust 2 cookie sheets with flour.

Combine the dry ingredients in a bowl, make a well in the center, and pour in the oil. Add enough boiling water to form a firm but slightly sticky dough. Let rest for 5 minutes.

On a floured surface, roll out the dough to about 1/8-inch thickness and cut into 2-inch rounds with a cutter. You will need to add a little more hot water when rerolling the trimmings to keep the dough soft.

Put the crackers on the prepared cookie sheets; they can be positioned close together because they don't spread. Bake for about 20 minutes until crisp but not browned. Cool on a wire rack.

Makes about 32 crackers

variations

oatmeal chocolate chip cookies

see base recipe page 259

oatmeal raisin cookies
Follow the basic recipe, omitting orange zest and increasing the cinnamon to 1 teaspoon. Use raisins instead of chocolate chips.

oatmeal cranberry–orange cookies
Follow the basic recipe, using dried cranberries instead of chocolate chips. Reduce vanilla to 1/2 teaspoon and add 1 teaspoon grated orange zest.

dairy-free apple–raisin oatmeal cookies
Follow the basic recipe, but omit the egg and yogurt and replace them with 1 cup applesauce. Use only 1 cup oats.

gluten-free oat & chocolate chip cookies
Follow the basic recipe, substituting 1 cup gluten-free flour for the whole wheat and all-purpose flours. Ensure that the oats and baking powder are gluten-free too.

variations

strawberry shortcake

see base recipe page 260

apple & pear cobbler
Make the shortcake dough as instructed. Omit strawberries and the topping.
Prepare apple and pears as described on page 250 (up until roasting). Put in
a baking dish and top with the shortcake batter dropped in rough spoonfuls
over the fruit. Bake at 375°F for about 25 minutes until golden.

buttermilk biscuits
Make the shortcake dough as instructed. Omit strawberries and the topping.
Transfer the dough to a floured surface, roll out to 3/4-inch thickness, and cut
out 2-inch rounds with a cutter. Glaze with milk and bake on a flour-dusted
cookie sheet for about 15 minutes until risen and golden. Makes about 6.

angel strawberry cake
Prepare the strawberries as directed; omit shortcake. Serve the strawberries,
vanilla yogurt, and orange zest over 4 thin slices of angel food cake, page 262.

mango & passion fruit shortcake
Make the shortcake as instructed. Omit strawberries and orange zest. Serve
instead with the chopped flesh of 1 mango, the pulp of 2 passion fruit, and
the vanilla yogurt.

variations

angel food cake with blackberry coulis

see base recipe page 262

chocolate angel food cake with raspberry coulis
Follow the basic recipe, but use 1/4 cup less flour and add 1/4 cup sifted cocoa powder. Make raspberry coulis by substituting raspberries for blackberries.

cherry angel food cake with lemon glaze
Follow the basic recipe, adding 1/2 cup roughly chopped maraschino cherries that have been tossed in 1 tablespoon flour and gently folding into the finished batter. Make a glaze by mixing 1/2 cup confectioners' sugar or powdered sugar substitute, 1 1/2 tablespoons lemon juice, and 1/2 teaspoon lemon zest; drizzle over cooled cake. Omit coulis.

spiced angel food cake
Follow the basic recipe, adding 1 1/2 teaspoons apple pie spice with the flour and 1/2 teaspoon almond extract with the vanilla.

angel mascarpone trifle
Make the angel food cake and lay slices in the bottom of a serving bowl (you will have slices left over). Drizzle with 1/4 cup orange-peach juice; top with 2 peeled and sliced peaches. Combine 1 cup each fat-free Greek yogurt and mascarpone cheese, 2 tablespoons confectioner's sugar, and 1/2 teaspoon vanilla extract. Spread half of the mixture over the peaches. Repeat with a second layer. Garnish with raspberries and mint leaves.

variations

skinny vanilla raspberry cupcakes

see base recipe page 263

skinny cinnamon apple cupcakes

Follow the basic recipe, but use brown sugar and 1 teaspoon ground cinnamon instead of vanilla. Peel and core 1 apple and chop into small pieces. Fold into the mixture after the flour has been incorporated. Combine 2 tablespoons each Demerara sugar and finely chopped pecans and 1/2 teaspoon cinnamon; sprinkle over cupcakes before baking. Omit raspberries.

skinny coconut raspberry cupcakes

Follow the basic recipe, omitting vanilla. Use just 1 cup flour and add 1/4 cup shredded coconut. Sprinkle a little extra coconut over the cupcakes and raspberries before baking as directed.

skinny rosewater & almond cupcakes

Follow the basic cupcake recipe, omitting vanilla and substituting 2 teaspoons rosewater. Replace raspberries with a few slivered almonds.

vanilla chocolate swirl cupcakes

Make the batter for the cupcakes and divide in half. To one half add 2 tablespoons cocoa powder and sufficient milk to make it the same consistency as the other half. Put 2 tablespoons of each batter in the cupcake liners and swirl together with a thin-bladed knife. Bake as directed.

variations

zucchini cranberry bread

see base recipe page 265

zucchini, ginger & walnut bread
Follow the basic recipe. Use 1 1/2 teaspoons ground ginger and 1/4 teaspoon ground cloves instead of cinnamon and nutmeg. Add 1/2 cup chopped walnuts instead of cranberries, and orange zest and juice instead of lemon.

carrot bread
Follow the basic recipe, using shredded carrots instead of zucchini. It works well with half carrot and half zucchini too.

zucchini chocolate bread
Follow the basic recipe, using only 1/4 cup cake flour and adding 1/4 cup sifted cocoa powder. Add 1/2 cup semisweet chocolate chips instead of cranberries.

strawberry banana bread
Follow the basic recipe, omitting zucchini and adding 1 medium banana and 4 ounces strawberries, mashed together. For the spice mix, use 1/2 teaspoon each of cinnamon and cardamom and a generous pinch of nutmeg.

variations

lemon roulade

see base recipe page 266

lemon poppy seed roulade
Follow the basic recipe, adding 1 1/2 tablespoons poppy seeds with the flour.

lemon & rosemary roulade
Follow the basic recipe, adding 1 teaspoon finely chopped fresh rosemary with the flour.

chocolate roulade
Follow the basic recipe, omitting the lemon zest and oil. Use only 1 1/2 cups flour and add 1/2 cup sifted cocoa powder. For the filling, use vanilla-flavored yogurt instead of lemon.

jelly roll
Follow the basic recipe, replacing the filling with 1 cup sugar-free preserves such as raspberry, cherry, or apricot.

variations

orange polenta cake

see base recipe page 268

upside-down orange polenta cake
Put 1 tablespoon low-fat butter and 2 tablespoons sugar-free maple syrup
into a small pan. Bring to a boil, stir, and pour into a prepared 9-inch cake pan
(do not use a loose-bottomed pan as the syrup will leak out). While still hot,
arrange a layer of thin orange slices over the bottom of the pan, cutting them
as necessary to cover the pan. Make the cake batter as directed, spread over
the orange slices, and bake and cool as directed. Slide onto a plate to serve.

orange coconut polenta cake
Follow the basic recipe, adding 1/2 cup unsweetened flaked coconut with
the flour. Omit cardamom.

orange blueberry polenta cake
Follow the basic recipe, adding 1 cup fresh or frozen (unthawed) blueberries
that have been tossed in 1 tablespoon flour.

orange polenta cake with orange-flower water syrup
While the cake is baking, make a syrup by combining in a small saucepan
the juice of 1 orange, 1/2 cup sugar or sugar equivalent, and 2 tablespoons
orange-flower water. Bring to a boil and simmer, stirring, until the sugar
has dissolved. While the cake is still warm, prick the surface all over with a
toothpick and slowly pour over the syrup; cool.

pistachio & orange biscotti

see base recipe page 269

almond & cranberry biscotti
Follow the basic recipe omitting orange zest and juice. Use 1/2 cup whole blanched almonds, toasted, instead of pistachios. Add 1/4 cup dried cranberries along with the nuts.

pine nut & lemon biscotti
Follow the basic recipe omitting vanilla. Use 1/2 cup pine nuts instead of pistachios. Use 1 teaspoon lemon zest and 1 tablespoon lemon juice instead of orange zest and juice.

espresso biscotti
Follow the basic recipe omitting orange zest and juice, vanilla, and pistachios. Add 1 tablespoon ground espresso powder and 1/2 teaspoon ground cinnamon with the flour.

chocolate pistachio biscotti
Follow the basic recipe, adding 3 tablespoons cocoa powder with the flour. Omit orange zest and add 3 tablespoons skim milk instead of the orange juice (or, if desired, keep the orange juice and zest and add just 1 tablespoon milk).

pine nut & lavender biscotti
Follow the recipe for pine nut and lemon biscotti above, but add 1 teaspoon dried lavender buds with the flour and omit the lemon.

variations

craving for chocolate cake

see base recipe page 271

chocolate prune cake

Follow the basic recipe, using puréed cooked prunes instead of the applesauce.

mocha cake

Follow the basic recipe, omitting the coffee powder and adding 2 tablespoons very strong espresso to the applesauce mixture.

chocolate orange cake

Follow the basic recipe, omitting vanilla and adding 1 tablespoon grated orange zest. If liked, spread 2/3 cup sugar-free orange marmalade, which has been slightly warmed, over the cooled cake as a glaze.

chocolate cardamom cupcakes

Follow the basic recipe, adding 1 1/2 teaspoons ground cardamom with the flour. Omit vanilla bean or paste. Spoon the mixture into cupcake liners in muffin pans. Bake for 15–20 minutes, until a toothpick inserted into the center comes out clean.

variations

caraway oat crackers

see base recipe page 272

parmesan oat crackers
Follow basic recipe, adding 1/4 cup Parmesan cheese instead of
caraway seeds.

spicy lime oat crackers
Follow the basic recipe, using chili oil instead of olive oil and adding
1 teaspoon shredded lime zest to the dry ingredients. Omit caraway seeds.

sesame oat crackers
Follow the basic recipe, using 1/4 cup sesame seeds instead of caraway
seeds. Substitute 2 teaspoons sesame oil for 2 teaspoons of the olive or
canola oil.

seedy oat crackers
Follow the basic recipe, adding 2 tablespoons sunflower seeds, 1 tablespoon
each of flax and sesame seeds, and 2 teaspoons nigella seeds with the
dry ingredients.

index